Iron Soldiers in Vietnam

577TH ENGR BN
VIETNAM

Qui Nhon
Tuy Hoa
Dong Tre
Vung Ro Bay
Cam Ly
Nha Trang
Duc Trong
Cam Ranh Bay
Phan Rang
Da Lat
Don Duong
Saigon

Iron Soldiers in Vietnam

Richard F. Hill

For Those Who Perished

Contents

Iron Soldiers in Vietnam

Foreword

This book is a tribute to the men of the 577th Engineer Battalion (Construction) who served so honorably and courageously during that hellish time. And, this is also the story of the most interesting, and fascinating, year of my life. Now, and age 76, it was a *very* long time ago.

The year was 1967 and the place was Vietnam. I was 27 years old and the Commander of Company D, 577th Engineer Battalion (Construction), from mid-January until late July. I then took over Company C until mid November. Then I was as Assistant S-3 operations officer in Headquarters Company until my DEROS on 10 January 1968.

I have known for long time how important that period is to me, but when I went to the reunion of old comrades, I found out how important it was to them as well. About 125 people attended the reunion, including spouses and some families. The age of the men ranged from mid 60s to late 70s and gray hair, missing limbs, bad backs and canes were the order of the day. Everyone enjoyed those few days, even though we didn't remember who most of who the others were. We had a great time, telling our stories, drinking beer and booze, and just being together. But now, over a year later, it is time to tell some of those stories, along with mine.

A great many people worked on the projects I was fortunate enough to direct, including men from:

- A Company, 577th Engineer Battalion (Construction)
- B Company, 577th Engineer Battalion (Construction)
- C Company, 577th Engineer Battalion (Construction)
- D Company, 577th Engineer Battalion (Construction)
- Headquarters Company, 577th Engineer Battalion (Construction)
- 513th Engineer Company (Dump Truck)
- 553rd Engineer Company (Float Bridge)
- 572nd Engineer Company (Light Equipment)
- 2d Platoon, 643rd Engineer Company (Pipeline)
- 91st Evacuation Hospital and all the other self-help units

Is this book precise? No, not really. That year was so busy for me that I can recall only a few of the names of those two thousand plus men and women I proudly served with. For that I sincerely apologize. Some names herein were obtained from after action reports, battalion and larger command listings, and even Special Forces team listings. And my time-line may not be quite accurate either. (Getting old sucks...) But, I will point out that for the first 10-½ months of the tour there were so many projects and incidents occurring simultaneously that I decided to write about each separately, hopefully in a fairly close date sequence.

Most of what is discussed herein occurred during 1967 and early 1968. Much more occurred in the battalion after that, but others will have to write those stories. There is information about the war in general and about Agent Orange and other defoliants sprayed by C-123s, Hueys, Riverine Patrol Boats, and by hand. Nearly all our brothers are affected by Agent Orange.

The photos are mine, or have been donated, pulled off the battalion's Facebook page, or off the web. The quality may be poor as many were scanned, but words alone are not enough to tell this story. No copyrights have been intentionally violated. Any errors or omissions are entirely my fault.

The following is a quote from **FM 5-1 ENGINEER TROOP OR-GANIZATIONS AND OPERATIONS, which** describes how the various types of engineer units are organized and explains their wartime missions. This quote describes the mission of an engineer construction battalion. *"The great volume of engineer construction and rehabilitation work in the communications zone of an active theater of operations demands numerous construction and construction support units of varying types. These construction and construction-support units support the combat forces by construction and allied activities in the **rear areas**."*

Those last two words were a joke in Vietnam. The 577th operated in an active combat area, generally without infantry support. Very little of what we did was "by the book" and most of the men did many jobs for which they were not trained, especially those normally done by specially trained combat engineers.

To help memories, see Appendix F - Military Slang and Abbreviations if you don't get the meaning of some wording.

AND NOW

"IRON SOLDIERS"

"Get yer ass in gear and start shoveling"

Introduction

Phu Yen Province

During the period discussed in this book, the main body of the 577th Engineer Battalion operated in Phu Yen province along the central part of the Republic of Vietnam.

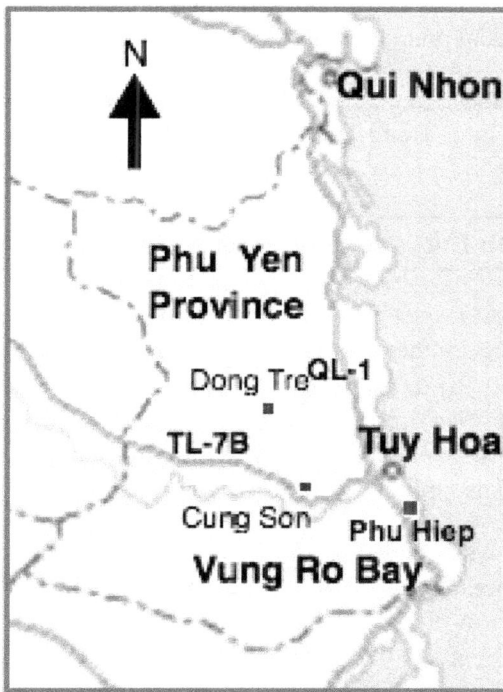

[1] "Composed of six districts and the provincial capital of Tuy Hoa City, Phu Yen Province included three main highways and thus served as a strategic transit hub north of Saigon along the coast. Historically, Phu Yen was a bastion of insurrection. A large percentage of the province's population aided the Viet Minh during the First Indochina War against the French.

By the time of the American war in Vietnam, 370,000 people called Phu Yen home. In late 1964, the People's Liberation Armed Forces (PLAF), or Viet Cong (VC), commenced its take over of Phu Yen with the mining of the railroad that transited the province. Eventually, the soldiers of the People's Army of Vietnam [PAVN, aka NVA - *Ed.*] Supported the PLAF. Within a year, the PLAF controlled approximately 90% of the province; resulting in the deployment of American and South Korean troops there to assist South Vietnamese forces. Sent to protect the rice paddies of Phu Yen were the American 1st Brigade, the 101st Airborne, and a regiment of Republic of Korea (ROK) marines. Over the next two years, those Allied contingents–supported by elements of the First Cavalry Division, the 4th Infantry Division, and the ROK 26th Division–participated in tactical operations in Phu Yen.

By 1967, these units opened QL-1, the nation's most important highway, from Nha Trang to Qui Nhon for the first time since January 1965."

577th Engineer Battalion Area of Operations

The 577th AO extended from the northern border of Phu Yen province down to the southern border below Vung Ro Bay. Major operations were from Vung Ro to north of Tuy Hoa on Highway QL-1 and east to the South China Sea coastline. The special forces outposts at Dong Tre near the northern boundary and Cung Son some 30 km to the south of Dong Tre were also major project locations

[2] "The area was opened by the 101st Infantry Division, a regiment of Republic of Korea (ROK) marines, supported by the 39th Engineer Battalion (Combat) in the summer and fall of 1966; in part to deny the rice harvest to the local VC. 4th Infantry Division elements were in the area during the monsoon season of 1966 - 1967. Actions of these combat units were thought to secure the area permitting 4th Infantry Division's relocation to Pleiku.

By April of 1967 the only remaining friendly forces in the Tuy Hoa Valley area were the 39th, the 577th, logistics units of the Tuy Hoa Subarea Command, the 6/32 Artillery Battalion, MACV advisors, 2 Light Helicopter companies, 1 Chinook CH 47 Medium Lift Helicopter Company, 1 ROK Infantry Battalion, and 1 ARVN Battalion. The ROK Tiger

8

Division Theater of Operations was from the Đà Rằng River (the largest river in Central Vietnam [which flows through Tuy Hoa - *Ed]*) north; while the ROK White Horse Division operated south of the river. Special Forces camps were located at Dong Tre and Cung Son.

Enemy elements were initially VC local and main force units. During the spring and summer 1967 NVA units began infiltrating in force from Cambodia and Laos down Route 7B through Cheo Reo. At that time Route 7B was considered open only from Tuy Hoa to Cung Son. West of Cung Son the road became barely distinguishable from the air and diffi-cult for vehicular traffic. Tuy Hoa Air Force Base had tactical fighter wing aircraft, mainly F-100's. These supported allied operations after contact had been established.

Route 7B

Route 7B extends from Pleiku in the central highlands to Tuy Hoa on the coast, a distance of some 135 miles, and was considered insecure from 2 km West of Tuy Hoa. Bridges: Only one bridge near Tuy Hoa, an old French class 12c Eiffel on QL1, was in place and permanent. [The class indicates a wheeled vehicle weight of no more than about 28.000 lbs - *Ed*.] All other bridges north and west of Tuy Hoa were blown; but the underlying streams were fordable during the dry season. A military topographical map of the time indicates that 7B is a good secondary road, which is misleading. At best, it was a 3 meter wide; mainly soil surfaced, occasionally with patches of gravel or river run rock; and was flanked by a canal which was approximately 15 meters wide. The canal flowed at a rate of 5-6 feet per second and was up to 3 meters deep. The canal was undamaged as it carried water for the entire Tuy Hoa Valley. It was a vital element of the rice harvest. Even the VC refrained from dam-aging it.

The pass approaching Cung Son from the East was steep and narrow with very thick vegetation on each side of the road. The vegetation was 8-10 feet high, providing excellent concealment. A 2 km area around the Cung Son special forces camp and the adjacent Montagnard village was considered secure."

It is interesting to compare the above analysis with the comments of Bernard B. Fall in *Street Without Joy*.[3] "Without respite, the G.M.

[French Army Groupment - *Ed.*] was now thrown into the difficult operation of reopening Road 7, and keeping it open over a distance of more than 70 miles in the direction of the South Annam coast, where a naval landing operation was to inaugurate Operation "Atlante" on January 20 [1954 - *ED*]. In the stifling heat, the men of G.M. 100 worked slowly and methodically, de-mining an always empty road and reconstructing bridges blown up by an invisible enemy."

Rules of Engagement

The area from Tuy Hoa west to the mountains, one could fire only if fired upon. The same applied from Tuy Hoa south past Vung Ro Bay. The area from the mountains to Cung Son was a free fire zone, meaning any Vietnamese could be engaged on site, day or night. Some of us did not always follow the rules, preferring to shoot first, protecting our troops, and then worrying about questions later, if ever.

Enemy Elements Deployed near Route 7B

The 377B Local Force was located in the Southern Phu Yen Mountains; for many years. The 30th Main Force Infantry Battalion was located in the Northwest Tuy Hoa Valley. Elements of the 95th Regiment operated in and out of the valley throughout the year.

Friendly Forces Deployed Along Route 7B

The 44th ARVN Infantry Battalion was deployed in the Northwest valley. Fire support bases were located at Chop Chai Mountain near Tuy and near Phu Hiep, approximately 25 miles to the South. Special Forces A-Team 221 with CIDG was located at Cung Son. Special Forces A-Team 222 with CIDG was located at Dong Tre. A limited numbers of Popular Force and Local Force units were deployed in the Tuy Hoa valley hamlets.

ROK Infantry Companies were deployed along Route 436 and in the vicinity of Phu Lam. The Koreans normally operated quite independently and did little to keep the 577th S-2 informed.

Generally speaking, the 577th Engineer Battalion operated without infantry support the vast majority of the time.

[1] "After the 1968 Tet Offensive, and subsequent Allied mop-up operations, a false sense of tranquility spread throughout much of the province. Except in the densely jungled interior of the province, the VC maintained a low profile in Phu Yen. Despite incurring heavy casualties during the 1968 Tet Offensive, the PLAF proved anything but defeated. Rather, the PLAF merely reverted to the first phase of Mao Zedong's Revolutionary Warfare doctrine. In that vein, as soon as 1969 the PLAF ramped-up abductions, assassinations, and attacks against Government of Vietnam (GVN) assets in the province. By 1972, PLAF continued its incursions into various villages, particularly those in Tuy Hoa District, the interdictions of the province's roads. Indeed, by the time of the Paris Peace Accords in 1973, American officials lacked knowledge of just how much of Phu Yen truly existed in a pacified state under the GVN."

References

[1] Robert Thompson, www.thompsonwerk.com/2014/01/phu-yen/, (2014-2015)

[2] Kenneth D. Jobe, Route 7-B Tuy Hoa to Cung Son, Phu Yen Province, (March 1968)

[3] Bernard B. Fall, Street Without Joy, (1961), 189

Iron Soldiers in Vietnam

Chapter 1 - Arriving

---

14 Jan 1967

It was a long flight from Fort Lewis, WA, To Hawaii, and then Taiwan, where the crew was swapped out for the remaining hop to Vietnam. The plane, a chartered stretch Boeing 707, was at about 15,000 feet when I looked out the window over Saigon. I knew that our destination, Bien Hoa airfield, was only about 25 miles northeast. I wondered why we were still so high when I noticed that the stewardess was so nervous that she had 3 cigarettes and 2 cups of coffee going as she sat in the galley. Something was not quite right.

Then the pilot nosed the plane down hard in a tight circle over the airfield, finally coming in hot and fast. The plane quickly taxied to the "terminal" and we began offloading through the front door. Down we came in our wrinkled khaki uniforms, while at the aft door the planeload of GI's going home were turning in their rifles as they boarded in dirty fatigues. They boarded fast and it seemed just minutes until the 707 took off.

Then I heard the sound of mortars just outside the perimeter at the west of the runway. The base was under attack. I felt naked, with no weapon, standing there not knowing what to do. A Vietnamese Air Force (VNAF) T-28 fighter bomber was next in line on the runway. These were former USAF and USN flight trainers converted for that use.

So much ordnance was hanging under the wings that they seemed to sag. The pilot, wearing a white silk scarf like the Red Baron, was revving up the engine, which sounded not so sure of itself. Soon, he let go the brakes and sputtered down the runway, belching smoke and oil. He then stopped, turned around, went back and repeated the drill, but this time he made it into the air. And, right over the perimeter, he dumped his entire load of bombs. The plane leapt skyward from losing so much weight, and immediately came around the runway and landed for another load.

The T-28's had been around as a fighter bomber in Vietnam for a long time. The U.S. Air Force used them in the 1950s in support of the French forces fighting the Viet Minh in the first IndoChina War

We were quickly herded into a tin building and sorted out by assignment. I was headed for the 45th Engineer Group in a place called Qui Nhon, wherever that was.

About then a grizzled Air Force Sergeant arrived and started calling out names. Several of us were directed to a C-123 and we were off to whatever awaited, wherever we were going. Being "combat loaded" into the C-123 meant "put your bod wherever you can." I ended up on a pallet of ammunition boxes as we flew around Vietnam all afternoon, delivering supplies and people. I was tired from the long flight over the Pacific and soon got used to the frequent landings and takeoffs, falling into a sound sleep. A long day transitioned into night.

Suddenly, I awoke to see fire rushing down the both sides of the aircraft! Just before entering a full scale panic, I realized that the flames were landing lights on the runway! Diesel oil, burning in sand-filled 55 gallon drums. Welcome to Qui Nhon Army Airfield in the lovely land of the 'Nam.

Getting A Job

The next day I was taken to the headquarters of the 45th Engineer Group for my real assignment. COL George M. Bush, the commanding officer, left me perched on a metal chair outside his office door for several hours. Inside, I could hear him coordinating an unsuccessful search effort for Michèle Ray, a young and beautiful French journalist who had been captured by the Viet Cong that morning.

Apparently, she had visited his headquarters, and him, the previous evening while on an adventurous attempt to drive from the Company D to the DMZ. Her car was later found with a flat tire and heavily booby trapped with a hand grenade and 155 mm artillery round. The Viet Cong freed her unharmed after several weeks. She reportedly became converted to their cause.

After a couple of hours, I was told to come in. Upon reporting to him, he asked me what kind of job I wanted. I said, "Company commander of a combat engineer company."

He said, "And if you can't have that?"

15

I said, "Assistant operations officer in a combat engineer battalion."

He said, "And if you can't have that?"

I said, "Company commander of a construction engineer company.

He said, "And if you can't have that?"

I said, "Assistant operations officer in a construction engineer battalion."

At this point COL Bush said, "What the hell, Hill? Are you trying to be typical?"

"You asked, sir" I replied.

He assigned me to take over Company D of the 577th Engineer Battalion (Construction), replacing CPT Ed Starbird, who had brought the company over from Fort Benning, GA, and who was finishing up his 6-month stint as a commander. The 577th was located at Phu Hiep, about 25 miles south of the provincial capital of Tuy Hoa, in Phu Yen Province.

"Batman" (his call sign) frequently visited our battalion until it was transferred from the 45th to the 35th Engineer Group. He had a reputation for chewing out nearly every officer he met, but I never had a problem with him.My cohort in crime, CPT Ken Jobe, who had flown over with me, had spent an entire week at the Replacement Battalion, fighting for a job he wanted. He refused a USARV staff position, A MACV Chief Well Drilling Detachment C.O., and several other equally glamorous positions. He kept saying, "I want my company back. The same one I had at Fort Benning, Company C of the 577th Engineer Battalion. I didn't come to Vietnam to sit behind a desk. I am a company commander!" The personnel E7 finally got tired and gave him a ticket on that same C-123 after telling him Company C was in Vung Tau, a resort area. Ken sang the same story at the 18th Engineer Brigade and was sent on to Qui Nhon to face COL Bush at the 45th Engineer Group. Ken told him that he needed to get his company back. Bush gave him Company B of the 577th. Now he just had to figure out where Tuy Hoa was and how to get there.

Chapter 2 - Phu Hiep (Jan - Jul)

Upon arriving at the 577th Engineer Battalion (Construction), located at Phu Hiep, right on the South China Sea, I reported to MAJ Frank Maturo, the acting C.O. of the battalion. I found out later that the new C.O. was LTC Carl P. Rodolph, who was then the brigade engineer of the 173rd Airborne. His orders said he was to assume command on 23 December 1966, he but didn't show up until February. The 173rd Airborne Brigade was planning a combat jump in Operation Junction City and Rodolph wanted to participate. He was also very upset that he was not offered a combat engineer battalion. After several weeks he was told to go on up the 577th and take the command, or lose it. He missed the 22 Feb jump. Sorry, Boss, no combat jump star on your wings.

The official name of the area in which we were stationed was the "Free World Forces (FWF) Cantonment Area" which was a rather ridiculous sounding name for a big sand pile. So, I'll just call it our base camp and let it go at that.

The 577th was a reinforced engineer battalion comprised as follows: The 553rd Engineer Company (Float Bridge), the 572nd Engineer Company (Light Equipment), Company B and Company C, of the 39th Engineer Battalion (Combat), and one section of the 513th Engineer Company (Dump Truck) were attached to the battalion. A platoon of the 643rd Engineer Company (Pipeline) would be added later

Company C of the 577th was detached from its parent soon after the battalion arrived in August of 1966 and was currently located in the delta several hundred miles to the South.

Battalion headquarters, Company A, one platoon of Company B, Company D, the 553rd Engineer Company (FB), the 572nd Engineer Company (LE) and the dump truck section were operating in the base camp at Phu Hiep. Company B (-) was stationed at Port Lane on Vung Ro Bay. Company B of the 39th Engineers was located at Tuy Hoa north and Company C, 39th Engineers was at Ninh Hoa. A task force was at Cung Son. The battalion and attached units were all part of the 45th Engineer Group.

You could call it the 577th Engineer Battalion (Construction) (Heavy). Lots of folks.

If memory serves, the officers of Company D at the time I assumed command were:

- First Lieutenant William Douglas Booth, Executive Officer

- First Lieutenant Theodorus C Veenhuis, Earthmoving Platoon Leader

- Second Lieutenant Edward A Brown, Construction Platoon Leader

- Second Lieutenant Edward A Meehan, Construction Platoon Leader

- Warrant Officer Clovis D Steelman, Maintenance Officer

Here is how a construction company was organized:

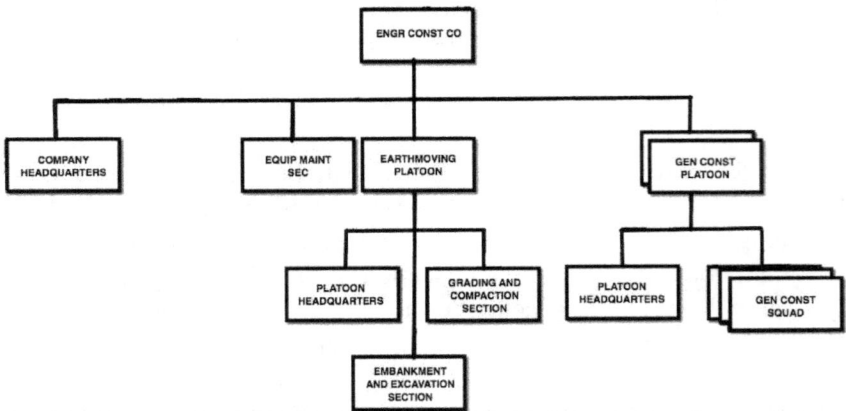

This was home for about five months

91st Evacuation Hospital

One of the projects of Company D was construction of the 400-bed 91st Evacuation Hospital. The work had been started on 17 December 1966 under the command of CPT Starbird, opened in 15 March 1967, was completed on 17 June, with nearly 160,000 man-hours of work.

The weather was really lousy until March, it still being the monsoon season. The men worked in high winds and driving rain to ready the hospital for its first patients.

Like most of our structure projects, this one was self-help. That meant that the lower ranking medics and administrative staff from the 91st got some carpentry skills and learned how to shovel sand, cement and aggregate into a small concrete mixer.

Batch Plant

For some reason, the Army had long before decided that two 16 cubic foot concrete mixers, shovels and wheelbarrows were adequate for an engineer construction company. But we needed a lot more than that, as the project included 74 buildings on concrete slabs, plus a mile and a half of covered sidewalks.

Since nothing else was available, I decided that we would just have to build our own concrete batch plant. A hole in the sand was dug by one of our dozers. It was about 9 or 10 feet deep, with a long sand ramp at either end. The sides were reinforced with heavy timbers and a roadway of PSP (pierced steel plank) was laid down to keep trucks from getting stuck. On either side were three timber-walled areas to contain sand, cement and aggregate. A 16-S mixer sat in front at the edge above the roadway on each side.

The tailgates of two 5-ton dump trucks were removed and a makeshift chute was welded in place. The trucks would drive into the pit and both mixers would dump concrete into the truck bed. When filled, the truck would drive to the current work site and dump the concrete. Meanwhile, the other "ready mix" truck was being filled.

Needless to say, the batch plant was an extremely labor intensive operation. The cement came in 80 lb sacks from a plant in South Korea (paid for by the U.S.). The sacks were split open by a shovel and dumped on a pile. The aggregate came from the quarry and crusher operation run by Company A, and the sand came from all over the area. The sand, cement and aggregate were then shoveled into the mixer along with water that was pumped in. It was all was powered by a small gasoline engine for each side of the "plant."

Engineer troops are very smart and always look for the most efficient (read "easy") way to do things. Therefore, we showed the medicos what to do and had them do most all the manual labor, which certainly seemed fair to us. Why should they just sit around while we built their hospital?

And, if a mixer was not cleaned out at the end of the day, the leftover concrete would quickly harden under the tropical heat. Not good. To clean it, the operator was required to get inside the mixer and break the concrete up with a 3 lb sledgehammer. Imagine being inside a bell and ringing it for about 30 minutes. No one ever had to clean up this way more than once.

Of the 74 buildings, 4 were surgical and intensive care, one was a large mess hall, and the remaining 69 were 20' x 100' SEA huts (Southeast Asia huts). These were patient wards, barracks and office buildings. Not on the official list was a smaller hut that was specially built for a male and female nurse who got married while we were building. So they got a honeymoon hut. Engineers at work, off the books.

The surgical and ICU buildings were each made of two steel quonset huts that were raised and set on concrete walls about 3 feet high. Some 16 surgeries could be performed simultaneously. It was truly an awesome place.

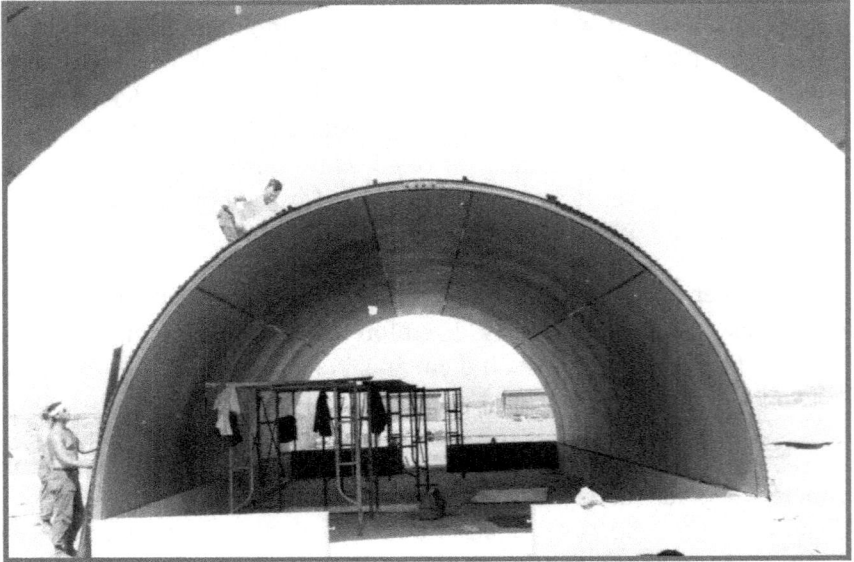

This is a surgery under construction and the picture below is one that is finished. Crude though they looked, one of the doctors told me that they were almost as good as those at Walter Reed Army Hospital in DC.

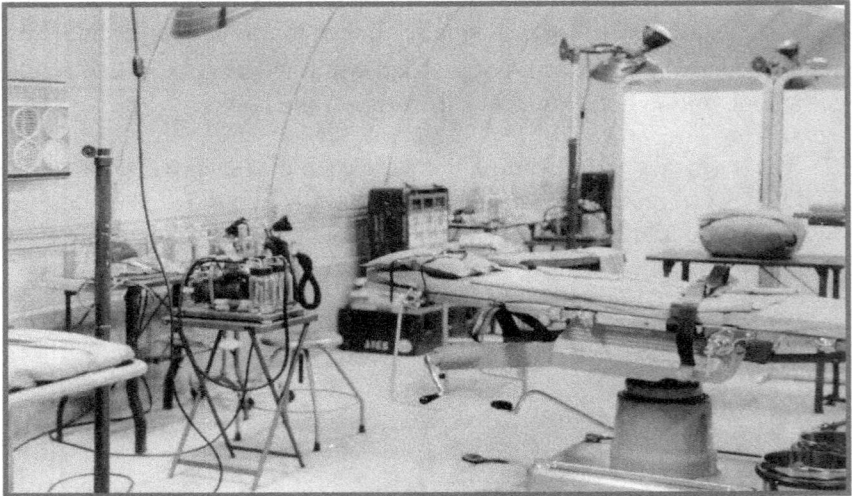

Initial Opening: 3/15/1967

There was a grand opening ceremony on 15 March, well before the actual finish date. This was held just outside the entrance to the newly operational surgeries and opposite the helipad. The folks from the 91st were on one side and about 30 of our guys were on the other side. The C.O. of the 91st gave a really great speech in which he explained how his men had built the entire hospital without any help! Behind me, I could hear grumbling and feel the anger rising. A riot, maybe? Yeah, we needed a good riot.

But just then a group of Dustcff choppers started landing. The folks from the 91st went into action while we stood and watched many seri-

ously wounded soldiers from the 4th Infantry Division being rushed into the surgeries. The division had been in a major firefight during the night and this was the price they had paid.

I turned and looked at my men. As far as I could tell, there wasn't a dry eye in the bunch. Mine as well.

Temperature Time

Not long after that, I was checking on some power problems and went into the ICU. There was an MP sitting on a chair at the end of a bed, his pistol drawn and cocked, facing the North Vietnamese prisoner in the bed. He was carefully guarding a man who had no arms or legs!

I ordered him to safe his weapon and put it back in his holster. It would have been really funny if it had not been so serious. And, as this was going on, a senior nurse came in. She said the prisoner would bite off the thermometer every time his regular nurse tried to take his temperature. She tried twice and he bit the thermometer off and spat it out both times. Then she grabbed his body, flipped him over, and shoved a third thermometer up his butt. When she flipped him back over, he indicated that he would be a good boy from then on. After his recuperation, he would have been turned over to the Vietnamese police (the White Mice). I doubt he survived their tender care and torture.

The nurse was Lieutenant Colonel (then Major) Annie Ruth Graham. She was the Chief Nurse. Annie suffered a stroke in August of 1968 and was sent to an evacuation hospital in Japan where she died four days later.

Many Vietnamese were also treated at the hospital. In the 30 June 1967 edition of the Castle Courier newspaper I was quoted as saying, "The men don't say much about their work, but you can see the enthusiasm and pride in their eyes when and injured or sick child is treated and released from the hospital." The headline for the story was "Engineers Build Jungle Hospital." (Have you figured our that this hospital was not in the jungle, but on the beach at the South China Sea?)

The only thing wrong with the quote is that I didn't say it. That's literary license, I guess. I do recall taking a reporter from some publication around to several of the battalion's various projects. When we left the security of the base camp and were well on the way to Company A's quarry at Chop Chai Mountain north of Tuy Hoa, he suddenly remembered he had a plane to catch. Scared shitless he was. It was only just recently, while researching this book, that I discovered the quote. I'm famous!

Eric Sevareid

Speaking of correspondents, lets jump forward a bit over a year when I was a student (with Ken Jobe) at the Engineer Officer Career Course. There was a program of prominent guest speakers, most of whom were quite interesting. But one in particular was not, and that was Eric Sevareid who was pretty much the #2 talking head behind Walter Cronkite of CBS. The EOAC commander, an absolutely worthless colonel whose name I cannot recall, knew that the 100+ officers in attendance (all but one who had just returned from Vietnam) were not appreciative of CBS. That network was not presenting the war favorably (even if they were eventually proven right). Because he expected total silence during the Q&A part of the talk, the colonel handed out questions, which he ordered to be asked. I got one.

We were told, "What is correct, what is wrong, doesn't matter. The man is a guest. Treat him accordingly."

Well, Mr. Sevareid gave a boring, all-knowing speech that talked down to people who had lost soldiers and who had recently been risking their own lives. He was not appreciated, to say the least, and the expected silence followed a total lack of applause at the conclusion of his speech. COL whatshisname was furious and tried to coax questions. Nada. Then he said, "Captain Hill, don't you have a question to ask Mr. Sevareid?"

At this point I must point out that I had previously worked for this jerk and he was the reason I volunteered to go to Vietnam 5 months before I was scheduled to.

I had been in charge of a power generation course there at Belvoir. We were teaching everything from 1.5 kw to 400 kw generators, 24/7, 3 classes per day. They didn't even have complete uniforms for those poor bastards. They were all draftees and I got one class of McNamara's Project 100,000 to train street kids to be soldiers. I had to act as pay officer and one kid signed with an X. I failed the entire class. Got called on the carpet and reamed out by said colonel. He said I was supposed to pass from 87.5 to 91.5% of all students. I explained that not one of that class could do the math required, some couldn't read, and I wasn't going to send anyone out to electrocute themselves. He didn't like that and repeated the rules. No excuses.

The very next class were all electrical engineering students with at least 2 years of college. 100% passed. More carpet time. I was supposed to pass from 87.5 to 91.5% of all students and I had obviously overreacted to his previous rant. No excuses.

This was just before Christmas. I went back to the office, told my GS-12 assistant I was going to Vietnam, called my wife and explained the situation, called the Office of Personnel Operations and said I wanted to go right after New Year's. Then I went home for lunch. Some jobs just ain't worth a bucket of spit and I didn't want to be court-martialed for eventually punching that fool out.

So this is probably why COL Asshole remembered my name. Anyway, it was obvious I had to say something, so I stood up and said, "Mr. Sevareid, can you tell us why CBS is manufacturing news in Vietnam?" He blustered some answer and we were dismissed. *Some times you are the bug, and sometimes you are the windshield.*

Hot Concrete

After the 4 day period of nice weather at the end of the monsoon season, it got hot, really, really hot. One of our concrete trucks left the batch plant and went directly to where a pad was to be. He raised the dump bed and nothing came down the chute. The concrete was absolutely solid.

At that moment, MAJ Howard Guba, the battalion operations officer, or S-3, arrived and began to berate the driver who, according to the really angry major, had obviously left his truck and gone to the post exchange!

After explaining that I'd seen the entire trip from batch plant to pad, the major calmed down and we began to investigate. Once we looked at the bags the cement had come in, it was obvious. We'd been sent a shipment of what is known as "High Early" cement, meant for use underwater with a very fast setup time. So, with all that heat instead of very cold water, it was a wonder the concrete didn't set up while it was being mixed.

26

It took a jackhammer to crack the concrete in the bed of the truck, but it was back in operation fairly fast. We double checked the codes on the cement from then on but had no further problems.

Water Tower

Lieutenant Bob Herndon and the men of his platoon from Company B were tasked to Company D in order to build the very large mess hall for the hospital. He and his crew did a great job, including the building of a wooden tower 40 ft tall. This was to hold a 10,000 gal water tank to supply the entire hospital.

The tower was well under way when I had to fly to the headquarters of the 35th Engineer Group in Dong Ba Thin, across from Cam Rahn Bay. The engineer forces in Vietnam had been re-aligned and our battalion was now part of the 35th Engineer Group. I don't remember why I had to fly down there, but when I returned a day or so later, I checked on the tower progress.

The tower was completed, but the tank was sitting on the ground and fully assembled. I asked LT Herndon why. He said that he wanted to make sure we had all the parts. Well, that sounded okay, until I asked him if all the bolts had been torqued down. He said yes. When asked how he was going to get the tank up on top of the tower, he thought for a moment and said he'd use a crane. I pointed out that our truck mounted cranes would have to sling the tank and lift it at least 60 ft in the air to place it on the tower. Small problem. Even with boom extensions, the crane could not possibly reach that high. Herndon then suggested building a sand ramp and driving the crane up higher. Well, that obviously wasn't going to work either.

This was the only water tank like it in Vietnam at the time and we could not remove the bolts without damaging the tank. Leaving him to think it over, I went on to other work.

That night about 2000, I got a call from LTC Rodolph about the tank. I told him I was letting Herndon stew over it a bit. He then said, "No, I mean what are YOU doing about lifting that tank?" I got it. I asked when he wanted the job done, and he said, "By 0930 tomorrow." He was jerking me around, but he liked to do that with his officers. I also knew he meant it.

We had to use a CH-47 Chinook helicopter to lift the tank. There wasn't any other way. So, I called "Big Windy," the 180th Aviation Battalion which was based at Phu Hiep Army Airfield. Company D and half the rest of the battalion had built the aviation complex so it would be easy to get a bird. I got hold of the duty officer and told him my problem. I asked for the oldest and most experienced pilot they had. After explaining the mission, the pilot and I agreed that he would pick up the tank in a vacant field at 0830. Then I spent most of the night designing a sling for the tank. The guys in the motor pool put it together, and after moving the tank with a wrecker, I met the pilot at the field. The sling was connected and tank and the chopper lifted off. The tank flew really well under the Chinook. Too well. They flew that thing all around the area, for about 20 minutes.

Finally, they came in over the tower and went into a hover to set the tank down. All of a sudden the 100 knot wind from the dual rotors was causing the tank to bounce in the air and creating some serious vertical oscillation in the helicopter. The pilot pulled up, went around and tried again with the same results. He was coming in to try again when I got him on the radio and asked that he return to the field and set the tank down there. He did, and landed nearby.

They had nearly jettisoned the tank due to the very real danger of crashing. The copilot had a release button in his hand, as did the crew chief who had been looking through the port in the floor as he was bounced up and down. The pilot said that my telling him the tank was the only one in-country was all that kept them from dumping it.

Finally, we hooked a nylon bungee loop into the top of the sling and the tank lifted off again. And, at long last, the pilot and crew placed the tank gently on the tower within a few inches of the center.

Their must have been a thousand people watching all this, taking pictures and, I think, hoping for something to happen. Herndon and I breathed a sigh of relief.

LT Herndon took over B Co. on 5 Aug 1967 and later went on to a successful 29+ year career in the Army, rising to the rank of Brigadier General. His final assignment on active duty was as the Army's Director of Facilities and Housing. Way to go, Bob.

The 91st Evacuation Hospital was completed on 17 May 1967.

One Jeep Full

Shortly after the hospital was completed, I was on QL-1 early one morning near the bridge over the Song Ban Thach River. There had been some kind of explosion in the village of Ban Nham, just south of the river. This was a known Viet Cong village though little was being done about it at the time.

As it turned out, quite a few villagers had been injured and there was no transport to the hospital. Vietnamese civilians had little or no priority for Dustoff evacuation. So we loaded up my jeep and headed up to the 91st. I had an elderly woman in my lap who was in pretty bad shape and unconscious. Most of her clothes had been blown off.

When we arrived at the hospital, the medics began unloading the injured. Turns out there were 11 Vietnamese packed in there. I carried the old woman into the surgery and put her on an operating table. About then she woke up, realized she was almost naked and had a fit over being seen by a giant white man. Guess she wasn't as bad off as I'd thought.

So far as I know, the medical wizards of the 91st patched everyone up.

Thirteen people in one jeep? Who'd thought it possible?

The 577th is in foreground and the 91st Evac by South China Sea.
The Sub-Area Command is in the top left.

Sandstorm

Not too long after the dry season began, I stepped outside my tent and was amazed to see the Northwest sky red and black up to perhaps 10,000 ft, or more. As soon as I realized it was a sandstorm, we spread the word to take cover behind the sandbags around the tents.

When the bloody thing hit, the winds must have been well over 40 mph with near zero visibility. Fortunately, there was no real damage other than a tent blowing over and a ¾ ton truck tipping on its side. But what a mess it made. Everything had sand in every nook and cranny.

The picture above is not of that storm, but was taken from Wikipedia. Sure looks like it though!

Cung Son

There was a special forces camp at Cung Song, 50 kilometers north and west of the base camp. For one thing or another, someone from the 577th was always going out there. Getting there by road was never a safe thing to do, but we got good at it. The trick consisted of mine sweep teams that leapfrogged each other, moving fast, only looking for signs of disturbance on the dirt and gravel road. But most importantly, very few people knew about the trips, which kept the Viet Cong and NVA at bay.

The first time I went to Cung Son was with a small team to look at some problems with the C-123 runway there. It was a clay strip that was covered with T-17 membrane, a flexible material that came in rolls. The problem was that moisture was getting into the soil from an underground spring, causing problems. We all agreed that the best solution was to knock the top off two hills behind the camp and fill in the valley in between. The team leader at the camp thought the location would be too far away. It probably was, but the soil was just too wet at the current site.

That was emphasized when a C-7A Caribou landed and pulled into the aircraft parking area.

As we watched, the wheels suddenly stretched the membrane and the plane sank almost to the top of the tires. The pilot, a grizzled warrant officer, dropped the ramp and clambered out of the plane. There was no other crewman on board. He asked the team leader to have a truck pull up in front of the aircraft and back up quite close. Then he dragged a heavy chain out of the plane, hooked it to the nose wheel assembly and the towing pintle and the 2-½ ton truck.

The driver was a Montagnard who didn't speak English, but with gestures and hand movements the pilot indicated that the he started the plane's engines, the driver was to put the truck in low gear and floor it, and to keep it floored until the pilot signaled him.

Well, when those engines revved up, that little guy was terrified and did just as he was told. And, in just a few moments, the Caribou literally jumped out of the holes, and then stopped. Someone had to go to the truck to make the driver shut it down.

I was totally surprised at this whole operation, but it was pretty obvious the pilot had done it before.

A task force composed of elements from HHC and Company A, Company B, and the 572nd Engineer Co. (LE) moved to Cung Son in a tactical motor march on 27 April 1967 to rehabilitate the airfield. Several hundred cubic yards of material were removed from deteriorated areas of the runway, apron and taxiways. The excavations were brought to grade with select fill material, compacted and surfaced with T-17 membrane. The project was completed in 17 days. Multiple supply convoys were conducted along route 7B without incident.

B/69th Becomes C/577th

The Army was really in a hurt for engineers in Vietnam and the 69th Engineer Battalion was one of those formed to augment the force. By my count, at the peak of the war there were 37 engineer battalions in-country, plus 62 separate engineer companies that had specialties such as a float bridge, light equipment, or a dump truck company.

The 69th Engineer Battalion (Construction) was created from scratch and was shipped out within 92 days. A remarkable task in itself, but with delays in obtaining personnel and equipment, the amount of training time was minimal at best.

Since it was brand new, the 69th had no significant experience and most of their officers were from Air Defense Artillery or Armor, which were not in big demand in Vietnam, but each officer had an engineering degree of some sort. Unfortunately, they had not had normal training with the Corps of Engineers and had no previous experience in army engineer units. They were detailed to the Corps for 3 years, which did not make a lot of the officers very happy. Company B's commanding officer, CPT Joe Richardson, had been in Air Defense Artillery.

The 69th arrived in Vietnam on 2 May 1967. Company C of the 577th had been long detached from the battalion and was down in the delta. In order to give some in-country experience to the 69th, Company C of the 577th was integrated into the 69th, and Company B of the 69th was sent to the 577th in return. It arrived in Phu Hiep on 24 May 1967 and was re-designated as Company C of the 577th.

The other purpose for the shuffling of units was to help with a major problem that every unit in Vietnam had, that of people rotating home at just about the time they really knew their jobs. The units that came over as a whole, like the 577th and 69th, had the problem of most of their people leaving at the same time. That made it really hard for the FNG who came in as replacements. The experienced folks would leave at about the same time and new men would come in and have to learn from scratch. This was a critical issue throughout the war and was a far cry from previous wars where you stayed for the duration. Had that been done in Vietnam, the war probably would have had far fewer casualties and may have ended sooner.

Phu Hiep Army Airfield

This project consisted of a 3,500 ft runway, parallel taxiway and 41,000 sq yd aviation maintenance area, as well as helicopter revetments, and a 75 x 202 ft for hanger. The construction went on at the same time as the building of the hospital. Men and much of the heavy equipment from the entire battalion worked on it.

The runway was to be built on a soil-cement base and surfaced with M8A1 metal sections. The entire base camp area was sand, but even so, fill material was needed to level the area on and around the runway site. Conveniently, the western edge of the camp perimeter had a low hill line that could permit enemy troops to fire down on our soldiers. What to do? Bring in all the battalion's 22 cubic yard scrapers, remove the hill for the runway and simultaneously provide a good field of fire for defense.

Bones

Previously, there had been a Vietnamese cemetery on the hill, but it had been removed entirely, or so we thought. The scrapers began their work, watched frequently by a civilian who seemed interested in the work. After the 290-M scrapers got closer to his perch, I got a frantic call from our earthmoving platoon sergeant, "Captain, you gotta come out here. We got bones all over the place! Come quick!" (Or something like that.) Sure enough, there was a trail of bones behind a scraper that had spread its load. And right after that I got a message to come to battalion headquarters.

There I found our interpreter and the Vietnamese civilian. The interpreter told me we had scooped up the man's parents and he wanted compensation. There was no way that was going to happen, given his watching us approach the unmarked grave for so long!

The discussion went on for a few minutes and then I asked the interpreter how much of the amount requested was he going to get? He was shocked and embarrassed that I knew. Hell, that kind of thing was rampant. Anyway, I told the man, through the interpreter, that there would be no money, but we would construct two very nice coffins, painted red (the good luck color). He didn't want wooden coffins. They would rot too fast. Instead, he asked for two C-Ration boxes. They, of course, were heavy cardboard that was soaked in wax.

So, we sort of split the bones, the ones we'd been able to find, into two piles and put them into the boxes. There was no way we could tell Mom from Dad. Didn't matter, the guy was happy, even if he didn't get cash. The boxes are probably still in good shape, the bones long gone to dust.

Swimming Pool?

As things progressed, we were going to need a source of fresh water, so we put a scraper to work. As the hole got deeper a D-7 bulldozer was added to push.

How deep to go? Stop when the water level gets to the battery on the dozer. And that's what they did, digging a hole about 7 ft deep by 20 feet wide by 80 feet long, which filled with nice cool water. It was just begging to be used as a swimming pool!

But, in such a disease infested part of the world, it was best to check with the C.O. of the hospital, who specialized in tropical disease. Unfortunately, he said that the water would have typhus in it within a few days, so no one could swim in it, but it would be okay for construction use. After 4 days the water did test positive for typhus. We were all disappointed. A swimming pool...

Getting Started

The project was surveyed, filled, surveyed, graded, surveyed, graded... Saw a lot of the surveyors from Headquarters Company, including Richard Meckley who kept all our projects "straight." He surveyed the airfield complex at Phu Hiep, the hospital, the helipads and revetments, and later, the airfield at Dong Tre. Thanks, Richard, and to those who helped, whom I can't recall.

The next step was to lay down the runway base, which would be a foot of soil-cement, whose advantages include high strength and durability combined with low first cost, making it an economical material. About 90 percent of the material needed for soil-cement is in place, keeping handling and hauling costs to a minimum. Like concrete, soil-cement continues to gain strength with age. Because soil-cement is compacted into a tight matrix during construction, the pavement does not deform under traffic or develop potholes like unbound aggregate bases. Soil-cement is capable of bridging over weak sub-grade areas and is highly resistant to deterioration caused by seasonal moisture changes. A self-propelled roto-tiller that mixed the cement, sand and water.

Cement Lesson

The runway base consumed thousands of bags of cement while making a 10-inch layer of soil cement as the base level of the runway. At the end of each 10 hour shift, the bags for the next shift were laid out. When the security situation permitted, two shifts per day were the norm, working under lights at night. The empty cement bags were thrown aside to be burned, but before long we gave them to the villagers in the 3 Phu Hiep hamlets. They took both the small amount of cement and the paper of each bag for their own use. Saved collecting and burning the bags.

Unfortunately, human greed came into play, as it so often did in that part of the world. Coming out to the airfield at the end of the night shift, it was discovered that the locals were stealing full bags of cement. So, the next morning, as a few dozen small people were laboring under their 80 lb loads, we called them back without luck. Time for a lesson. We let them get down to the beach where they would turn into the villages. Then a small barrage of 40 mm grenades was showered down in front of the group and an M60 machine gun ripped up the sand behind.

The bags were dropped and the group started to run home, only to be stopped by nearby fire once again. A few shouts and some hand signals and they went back and picked up the sacks, returning them to where they were stolen from. Once again, the bags were burned at the end of each shift. Thus endeth the lesson.

37

A Mess of Generals

As a young lieutenant in Germany, one of my extra duties was that of mess officer. Since I had to learn how an Army mess hall worked, I was determined that we have the best one in the battalion. From that point on, it became a bit of an obsession with me, leading to some interesting visitors in later years.

It started when Brigadier General Charles M. Duke came to visit during the construction of Phu Hiep Army Airfield around April, shortly after his promotion and assuming command of the 18th Engineer Brigade. We were advised of his coming in advance, but when he arrived, he was in a small convoy led by a military police jeep with large chrome plated sirens blaring.

Briefing BG Duke, LTC Rodolph and COL Newman (35th Engr Gp C.O) on the runway of Phu Hiep Army Airfield.

After briefing him and showing him the airfield and hospital, I felt I had to say something about that jeep, even though it wasn't my place. As we walked along, somewhat alone, I suggested that it might be safer to fly in the next time he wanted to come up. He was interested, so I further explained my concerns about having the presence of a general officer so loudly announced to the Viet Cong. Apparently, he'd been told that QL-1 was secure, though it was anything but.

Anyway, he stayed for lunch in the Company D mess hall. Then, a week or so later, he showed up again, unannounced for a project update, and lunch. He began to show up every two weeks, getting a really formal briefing usually with just he and I driving around in my jeep or walking the projects. He wanted it that way so his entourage didn't get in the way and he could ask what questions he wanted. As close as a captain and general can be in the army, we became friends.

Duke always came in just in time to get briefed, and then go to lunch. Pretty soon, other generals started dropping in — just for lunch. I'm not kidding. We had such a popular mess that we had to set up a special area for visiting generals. The company commander was expected to be there, of course, when high ranking visitors arrived. Army protocol. But it happened so often it was interfering with my work and I had to beg off being available just for show. After all, they were only there for lunch in a great diner! Who needs a captain just sitting there?

It may also have been that, distance wise, Phu Hiep was just a convenient break for their frequent flights up and down the coast. But, we really did have a great mess hall. Wish my memory let me remember the name of the sergeant who ran it all. He had a tough job since we were serving 4 meals a day instead of the normal three. That's what happens with feeding two shifts per day.

It's also interesting to note that our mess sergeant and the NCO who ran the morgue at the 91st Evac became great friends. According to my sources, they kept their beer in the morgue cooler. Effective, but really weird.

Taking On The Heat And The Boss

It was unbearably hot working on the steel M8A1 matting. In the heat of the day, you could not stand in one place for very long. It felt like your boots were melting. And, one day in early summer, our First Sergeant came out to the airfield and told me that the one thermometer we had burst from the heat. The highest it would go was 130 degrees F. He asked if we really wanted to order another one. We agreed that it was pointless.

In this picture The runway is nearly operational. The taxiway, park- ing and maintenance areas are underway.

It finally got so hot that the heavy leather gloves the guys were using to carry the steel matting were not enough protection. We got firemen's gloves from the fire department at the Sub-Area Command. Many tasks simply had to be done in early morning or at night.

The temperature would drop to the 80's at night and many men were sleeping under poncho liners to keep warm. Sounds strange, but a 50-60 degree swing is a lot any way you look at it.

M8A1 matting is a solid corrugated mat, designed to minimize issues with foreign object debris (FOD) that became common with jet engine aircraft. The M8A1 mats were 12 ft by 22 in. (147 lbs) and were constructed from a single sheet of solid steel that contained no punch out's (like PSP matting). Each mat contained 4 corrugated channels along the length of the mat.

One major problem we faced was thermal expansion. Unfortunately, the huge temperature swings from 80 to 140 degrees were causing the crossover from the runway to the hardstand to actually buckle up. The mat should have settled back down when the temperature decreased during the night. Not.

Once the joints buckled they remained taut and elevated day and night. This was my problem to fix, of course. I contacted the manufacturer to find out the coefficient of thermal expansion while seeking a solution. They had no idea, saying the mat was built to government standards. Great.

One evening, between shifts, I was sitting on the runway with pen, paper and slide rule in hand. Yes, slide rule. It was months later until the S-3 shop got a Friden mechanical calculator. As for a computer? What's that?

Anyway, while I was being frustrated with the calculations, the battalion commander, LTC Carl Rodolph walks up. I stood up. No salute. We didn't do much of that. He asked me what I was doing. Well, I thought it was pretty obvious, but I told him. He then poked his finger in my chest and said something to the effect of, "What are you thinking?" I explained again what I was doing. He poked me again and said, "No, I said what are you thinking?"

Hmmm, I didn't like this and I didn't like where it is going. I told him again, as I had before. Damned if he didn't poke me a fourth time and said the same thing. That was it. I stepped back saying, "I thinking how far I'm gonna kick your ass down that runway if you touch me again."

He gave me a stern look and then laughed and said, "I thought so." Uncle Carl (my pet name for him) and I got on famously after that. He just liked to pick on his officers. I had noticed that every Monday, at the next day's planning meeting, he would single out one officer and give him hell about little or nothing. I think he liked the game, but he really wanted to know who would stand up to him. And, after the officer's planning meeting, the NCO's got together and figured out what was really going to happen the next day. The Army way, eh?

We figured out that the M8A1 solution was to cut the mat, lay it flat again, and then weld the edges together. In the 420 foot crossover six joints were buckled. Upon cutting the matting in three locations some 21 inches of matting had to be removed. The new seams were then welded. The final solution to the buckling problem was to only lay the matting in the daylight so that it would be expanded by the heat, and to stretch it every 50 ft by pulling it tight with a truck and chain.

Above photo is welding the M8A1 matting on a curve with power from the contact truck behind.

Here's a story from then Lieutenant Barry Frankel who was the S-1 (Adjutant): "Been having an interesting weekend remembering as much as I can from my days at the old 577th. I was only there for a few months - Feb thru Jun of 67...but those few months set me up for the next 48 years...That would be now, in my 15th year of retirement...during that whole period I have been wondering who owes me $98 plus interest for a rifle that I never lost. It has recently come to my attention that the real person who scooped the gun was my good friend CPT Hill...the tall one. So the way I see it, I paid Rodolph $98+ one morning and told him, in my own fashion, that I did not want to hear any more crap about that rifle. He never mentioned it, never paid me back (it was sitting behind his desk the whole time)...He became a great friend for the rest of my military career (3 yrs) and for twenty or so years of my thirty years as a civilian for the Corps in Washington (actually became a big shot). He's watching down on us now and laughing his ass off... So my only recourse is YOU...$98 capitalized at 3% interest for 48 years is a little over $500...a check will be fine."

Barry, it wasn't me, honest. I think it was Uncle Carl hisself. He'd do something like that.

And, just to show that things were quite serious at all times in head-quarters, shown below Are Lieutenants Frankel, Herndon and Bowers. The latter two were in the S-3 shop at the time, which must have been around May.

"Speak no evil, see no evil, hear no evil..."

Wrong Dong

About this time Company D had a large crew of civilian workers out on QL-1 filling potholes and trying to keep the road operational under the increasingly heavy traffic of military vehicles.

The workers were paid the grand sum of 100 Piasters (Dong) per day, which converted to about $1.25 per day. They were paid every day. The strange thing was that they always wanted to be paid in new money. Never did figure that one out.

Anyway, late one afternoon we got a frantic radio call from the jeep driver/RTO of the platoon leader who was in charge of the project. Essentially he said that LT Brown was in a heated discussion with the "boss" of the workers and just might get killed. The reason was that the money he had with hime to pay out was soiled, old and wrinkled.

This really was a serious matter and these two men were alone with 50 or so angry Vietnamese.

We quickly gathered all the new piasters we could round up in the battalion area and I took off in my jeep with a bag full of money. Fortunately, we got out there before anyone got hurt and made the payments.

I don't see anything wrong with old money. I'll take it any day.

A Jump and a Bump

Several of the officers in the battalion were jump qualified and one day the Boss asked us if we'd like to make a jump with Special Forces at their airborne training base for indigenous troops at Dong Ba Thin. Hell, yes, I loved jumping out of planes. Fantastic fun.

So, on 23 Jun we hopped a bird to Dong Ba Thin and got there just in time to put the chutes on and go. As I clambered into the rig which was, as always, too small for my long body, it dawned on me that it had been 4 years since I had last jumped. Hmmm, will I remember everything I have to do?

We boarded first, going to the front of the C-123, which would put us going out last. I think there were 4 of us, so we split to be the end of the "stick" on each side. The trainees, all Cambodians, were on their first jump, naturally nervous. They didn't speak English, but did understand the commands and hand signals of the jumpmaster.

As we approached the drop zone the jumpmaster, a big ol' Master Sergeant, gave the command to "Get Ready!" about 6 minutes out, followed by "Outboard Personnel Stand Up!" and "Inboard Personnel Stand Up! " The little guy beside me was terrified. He didn't stand up, so when the next command, "Hook Up," was given, I kinda pulled him up and hooked the static line for him. At least he was ready at "Check Static Lines!", which he did not do. At "Check Equipment" you are supposed to give yourself a once over and inspect the back of the man in front of you. My friend started pulling the rip cord!

45

As you can imagine, a parachute opening inside of an airplane is something way less than desirable. As the pins were being pulled from the chute, I wrapped my arms around him as an officer from the other stick began to put him back together. I think they skipped the "Sound Off For Equipment Check!" command, since the trainees probably didn't understand the response of "Okay!" Dunno.

The next command is "Stand In The Door!" with 10 seconds to go, this command tells the first jumper to take his position at the exit door, and those behind him to follow, and be ready. Yeah, right!

There is a light by the exit door. It is turned on at the 6-minute warning and is red. When it turns green, the jumpmaster makes a final visual check of the LZ and gives the command to "GO!", and the jumpers exit the aircraft as rapidly as possible. The plane is traveling at about 130 knots, and even the slightest delays causes big spaces. But, of course, these guys were sorta slow, it being their first jump. My friend, however, didn't want to move, but I did, and he was in front of me. So, I simply picked him up and ran him to the door, where the jumpmaster gave him a big smile, grabbed his harness, and threw him out the door.

Remember that light and what happens after it turns green, okay?

I exited the aircraft, checked my canopy to make sure all was well, and then noticed a strange situation. I was the last man out, but a dozen or so jumpers were actually above me! They were so light that the big 33 foot diameter T-10 chutes just followed the wind, or something. All I know is that they stayed up there so long that the next flight of planes had to abort to avoid running into the men. And each succeeding flight always comes in a bit higher than the previous just so they don't eat anyone. Some of the jumpers were actually going UP!

We made a second jump that day and Uncle Carl was given the honor of acting as jumpmaster since we were on the last plane and there were no more trainees to jump that day. We wore football helmets for a jump and he had been given a bright red one, close enough to Engineer scarlet. The red light came on red about 6 minutes out and he leaned out to start checking.

As the light turned green, Uncle Carl was out the door, and I followed right behind. But, you know why the jumpmaster makes that check? Cuz the pilot may not be right on the money. Well, as I floated down, I saw that we were over an ROK garbage dump full of open C-Ration cans. Actually, I couldn't see open cans at what was now about 800 feet, but I could see it was a dump and it certainly wasn't the drop zone.

To one side of the dump was the perimeter wire and, most likely, a minefield. Not good. To the other side was Cam Rahn Bay. That looked good, so I pulled one set of risers all the way down so that I was holding the silk, giving me a good sideways push. Not enough. I wasn't going to get a bath that day, and at about 50 feet off the ground I let go of the riser to descend normally, then I realized I hadn't rolled my sleeves down.

I could see Rodolph about 20 yards away and realized that the wind had suddenly picked up. Just before I landed, I saw him land and get jerked back into the air, then belly flop on the ground. And, as I landed, I was jerked off my feet and onto my stomach, being pulled by the wind through those open cans, the ones with the sharp edges. Because I was on my belly, it was impossible to hit the quick release for the harness located in the middle of my chest. After perhaps 50 feet, or so, I was able to roll over, but just as I hit the release, I crashed into a tree. A young Vietnamese kid ran up to me and said, "GI you make number huckin' ten landing!" I still have the scars on my arms today.

The Boss was really hurting, but he refused to go to the hospital in the area. We flew back to Phu Hiep and he went over to the 91st right away. Turns out he had pretty much dislocated something internally. Anyway, when he got back to work, I think the next day, he got a call from Brigadier General Duke who told him that the next time he made an illegal parachute jump, he should not wear a red football helmet that let the entire brigade staff see his performance. I don't remember if he told us, or if the story came "back channel" but it was a good laugh.

On 21 July we had the opportunity for one more jump. This was to be a ramp jump from the rear of a C-7A Caribou. We loaded up and I think we were all looking forward to a ramp jump. I remember that just as Ken Jobe leapt off the ramp, he pushed back with both arms as though he was exiting through a side door and pushing off to get out of the slipstream. As I moved aft for my turn, I thought he'd been brainwashed at

Fort Benning's jump school. Then I did exactly the same thing. Pushed right out that invisible door. Yep, it sure does stay with you.

Dong Ba Thin garbage dump. Richard Hill in foreground, Ken Jobe behind.

Surprisingly, we all were awarded the Vietnam Parachute Badge by the Luc Luong Dac Biet, the Vietnamese Special Forces High Command. Didn't know that was coming, but it did make us unique. The 577th Engineer Battalion was a "leg" unit, of course, and when the 173rd Airborne Brigade arrived in town, they were very surprised to see those wings. They were never awarded them and, to my knowledge, almost no one outside of Special Forces ever received them. The award was approved by the Army and I wore them proudly. Those wings and the 2 Meritorious Unit Citations that were awarded to the battalion are the only decorations that meant anything to me. Everything else personally awarded to me I considered as "been there" badges.

Two Boys Are Born

On 28 June I received a message from the Red Cross that my son Brian had been born back in Asheville, NC. Exciting news, of course, and I wanted to share it with CPT Larry Gralla who was the C.O. of A Company. His CP tent was just opposite mine across a dirt road. I started to run over to tell him the news, and we met right in the middle of the road. He was on his way to tell me that his son had just been born. Happy coincidence.

A few days later, we both drove up to Tuy Hoa AFB to make a phone call home to our wives. Anyone who has used the MARS (Military Affiliate Radio System) can appreciate the problems. MARS was designed to permit selected civilian short wave radio operators to receive radio messages from servicemen and the make a phone call to the recipient. They got no pay, but sometimes got surplus radio gear at no cost.

Anyway, when your turn comes up and a ham operator in the states has been reached, they make the phone call. When Momma answers, the ham explains the setup and tells her she must say "Over" whenever she wants hubby to speak. That, of course, is confusing to anyone not familiar with radio communications and so it works only in the last few minutes of the allotted time for the call. But it was nice to hear a voice from the world.

I was able to make one other call just before my DEROS. After returning home, I asked my wife what the calls had cost. There was no record of them on the phone bills. Weird.

My Dad was an avid ham operator and participated in the MARS system. He told me later that the reason we had never gotten the bill for the phone call (land lines, remember those?) was that Senator Barry Goldwater had paid for something like nine MARS stations and personally paid for all the calls made from them. Besides being a senator, he owned a chain of stores and thought that MARS offered a nice way to thank the troops in 'Nam. It was never made public that he paid for this. Thank you, sir.

Larry Gralla's men ran the quarry and rock crusher at Phu Hiep and continually provided the other units in the battalion with rock and aggregate for the various projects. Company A also was organized to have a tremendous maintenance capability. The line companies had excellent capabilities themselves, but for problems that would have ordinarily caused a piece of broken equipment to be sent back the states, Company A would fix it. It seemed there was nothing they could't fix. If parts needed to be made, they designed and made them.

Speaking of improvising, when we got 22 cubic yard Clark 290-M scrapers to replace older scrapers, we soon ran into a problem. The dry season dust was just too much for the air filters on the scrapers. To make matters worse, replacement filters were on backorder. That wouldn't cut it because we needed those scrapers.

Then I remembered someone laughing that the nurses in the 91st Evac had come over from the states with 2 CONEX containers full of Kotex. Hmm, that seemed like an awful lot. I made a quick visit and came back with a large boxful. We took the filter apart and replaced the contents with Kotex pads. Lo and behold, they were more efficient than the original! A little inter-unit negotiation and the problem was solved until the backorders were filled.

Wobbly Wheels Go Green

The civilian contractor at Tuy Hoa AFB lent me a wobbly wheel roller to use in building Phu Hiep AAF. They didn't ask for it back, so after a month so it somehow turned green all over and got some D/577 numbers on it. I think maybe CW2 Clovis W. Steelman, our maintenance warrant officer, just might have transmitted the infection which caused this moldy change to olive drab.

And, for some reason, one of the contractors at the AFB wanted to dispose of a pickup truck. He brought it to the dump where one of our dozers was working and asked that the truck be buried. The operator was amazed, but when assured it was okay, he asked if he could drive over it first and squoosh it. And he did. That story quickly made the rounds. Fun times.

Armed And Dangerous

Convoys were continually going to and from the supply depot at Cam Rahn Bay, and, occasionally there would be a breakdown of a truck.

It seemed that these usually happened on the return trip in the steep mountainous area south of Vung Ro Bay. When possible, Company B would retrieve the sick truck, but sometimes our maintenance crew would have to do it.

On one occasion, the First Sergeant and Operations Sergeant decided to go along for the recovery. Unfortunately, the team was ambushed, though not too seriously. According to the story told, our two fearless NCO's were lying on the edge of the road when one asked the other, "Where's your rifle?", with the reply of, "I forgot it. What about you?." A .32 caliber pistol was pulled out. Discretion being the better part of valor here, both men decided to hunker down until the show was over.

When the tale got out, there was a lot of laughter in the orderly room.

B52 Strike

As noted above, just about everything we worked with pretty much came from the depot at Cam Rahn Bay. And the trucks were heavily loaded on the return trip, so it was natural that would be when things broke. Here's another such instance when we got word of several break-downs.

CW2 Steelman and our wrecker and maintenance crew took off going south towards Ninh Hoa in the middle of nowhere. It was going to be difficult so I went along. We stopped at Vung Ro to get help from Company B. CPT Jobe, his Motor OfFicer, CW2 Hyde and Motor Sgt Sharpe added another wrecker, two 5-ton tractors with tow bars and logging chains. Everyone was heavily armed.

The young lieutenant who was the supply convoy commander was overjoyed to see us. After a quick hookup of the busted trucks, we headed back. It was a very dark night and going through the mountains south of Vung Ro was always dangerous. My gun jeep lead the way and Jobe brought up the rear, keeping an eye out for any bad guys who might try to ambush us from the rear.

It was late when we got up to Company B so I decided my gang would spend the night there and move on in the morning.

I was sleeping on a canvas cot in a tent when, at about 0200, there was a humongous roar and I found myself about a foot in the air above the cot. Crashing to the ground, it felt like an earthquake as everything continued to shake and bounce, though I soon realized it had to be a B-52 strike, and damned close!

There was supposed to be a 3 km safety zone around any such strike, but the next morning when I saw the tops of a couple of mountains missing, I knew we'd been only about 2 km away. Too close for me.

This Is My Push

A chapel was built for the battalion. Shown above is LTC Rodolph speaking at the dedication. The chaplain was CPT Emlyn Jones, who bore a resemblance to the Chaplain in the TV show M.A.S.H.

Shortly after beginning the first service, the battery powered podium speaker that the chaplain was using suddenly began broadcasting air force chatter from a bombing run by a nearby F-100. Without hesitation Chaps shouts out. "God, this is MY push!", and turned it off. He meant, of course, that it was his frequency, often called a push. The attendees loved it. A neat man with a great sense of humor.

He had wanted to make a parachute jump with us so Uncle Carl had pull-up bars built behind the chapel, and I recall trying to train him to make a parachute landing fall (PLF) by jumping off a CONEX container. After a while he changed his mind and we didn't even make him do pushups or run a few miles.

Chasing Charlie

Next to the Company D part of the battalion area was the Class II and IV yard, meaning where all the construction materials were stored until used. And in the company area was a diesel fired shower. One evening around 2100 there were 3 of our NCO's waiting for the water to heat. About 10 yards away I was availing myself of the P-Tubes, aka urinals made from tubing stuck in the sand and surrounded by lime, sanitation, y'know?

We were all attired in our evening shower best uniform, combat boots and white towels, when all of a sudden several shots rang out that were coming damned close. Too close. We all ran to get our M-16's and went towards the source of the shots, the II and IV yard. The troops, by the way, had all seemed to disappear. Smart.

We carefully entered the yard and started searching, but soon realized that white towels might not be the best combat uniforms. Okay, now it was 4 guys in nothing but boots and rifles. What a sight. Wow!

Before long we saw tracks in the sand. They were from a set of Ho Chi Minh sandals, which were made from old tires. One footprint had a hole in the sole. We followed the tracks around the yard and soon made a full circle, where we saw our own boot prints with newer holy sole prints on top. Yeah, exactly like a B-grade movie.

This parade went on for a couple of trips around the yard, but we were not getting close to Charlie. I wanted to drop someone off to shoot him on the next loop, but was worried that one of our brave (foolish?) group would be hit by accident.

After about an hour, or so, we had lost track of our bad guy, and gave up, hoping that he had skedaddled away. Very big mistake.The scene a few hours later was not good. Chuck wins this time.

Sometimes you are the windshield, sometimes you are the bug.

Phu Hiep School

Another of Company D's tasks was providing assistance in building a school in the village of Phu Hiep. The idea was that the USA would provide the materials and the inhabitants would actually build the school. That was the plan, but you know how plans went in Vietnam, right?

Two concrete block making devices were provided to help things along. They were simple molds that screwed in to compress concrete. The locals didn't like them, preferring to use wooden frames. Okay, no big deal. The men set to work under the supervision of a spec 5 and a spec 4. A few weeks after work started I made a return visit to the village. The women were doing all the work while the men watched, saying it was too hot for them to work.

The E-4 had rotated soon after, but the E-5 said he could manage. It was my fault for being too busy with other projects, but when I made my next check, no Vietnamese were working, just our guy by himself. When asked why he was doing that he said, "They won't work and I want to finish this project before I rotate." Obviously, he was very proud and didn't want to ask for help, knowing just how busy the rest of the company was.

Well, I was more than pissed at the villagers. So, after a bit of time on the radio making some arrangements, I went to the village chiefs (there were 2, brothers) and through the interpreter, told them I would destroy the school if they would not get back to work. In return, I received two inscrutable Asian smiles. They didn't think I was serious.

I gave a signal on the radio and, with that huge diesel engine roaring at top rpm, a D-7 bulldozer crashed through the heavy cactus barrier around the village. With black smoke blasting from the exhaust, the dozer charged into the village with the blade going up and down. It stopped about 10 yards in front of the school. I looked at the chiefs and dropped my hand. The dozer lowered the blade and started shoving a large pile of sand towards the school.

Thankfully, at that moment, the chiefs ran up saying that work would resume immediately. Needless to say, I was very pleased because I had no intention of destroying the building. It was very gratifying to see our young supervisor able to get back to work and, before long, see his project completed on 2 June 1967. Good job! I just wish I could remember your name.

Slick To Stick

Whenever the morning dew was on the M8A1 matting on the runway, it was slicker than greased owl shit. One day I made my jeep go completely around in a circle just by pushing on the left rear corner. I was really concerned about how any plane could land on it. But then people much smarter than me had it covered. And cover it we did with a special non-skid paint that gripped so much you had a hard time walking on it. Worked like a charm.

The last things we did before making the field operational was to paint runway numbers, centerline stripes and put in a portable landing light system. Ready to rumble.

First Landing

The C.O. of the 225th Aviation Company "Phantom Hawks" (OV-1 Mohawks) did not like the way the airfield was oriented, saying the wind was coming across the airfield and it would be dangerous to land. I replied that the wind in the area blew from every direction at different times, so it really didn't matter. He didn't like my response and demanded that I accompany him on the first flight in. Sorry, sir, but I don't fit into those planes. Too tall. That really torqued his props.

In reality, the strip was laid out parallel to the one at Tuy Hoa Air Force Base some 20 miles to the North. The weather was the same in both areas, so it truly made no difference.

This is the first OV-1 Mohawk to land at Phu Hiep AAF.

MAJ Howard Guba, our S-3 got "elected" to make the flight. He didn't seem too happy at the news, but liked the landing.

Amoebic Dysentery

Not long after the 225th arrived many of their men came down with amoebic dysentery. Apparently, they were exposed while still down in Bien Hoa but the outbreak held off until they moved. Not long after that the problem spread to those in our battalion base camp.

This was a severe problem and there was no quick fix other than absolute cleanliness and time. The hospital was overwhelmed, not being fully operational at the time.

So, it was decided that we would isolate the worst cases in one company where the mess hall got sanitized daily and the latrine shit cans burned frequently. In most cases, that worked well and after a couple of weeks the inmates of our little concentration camp got better.

The officers were another matter. We just kept going... and going... and going and...

We actually held a few staff meetings in a 6-hole latrine where the sitting positions rotated not on rank but on other pressures. My jeep was stocked with toilet paper and frequent stops were made on the roadside.

But, in time, all things passed.

Maintenance Area

In addition to the runway, Company D company, and all those who helped, built a 41,000 sq yd maintenance area, also out of M8A1 matting.

Revetments

Revetments were built from M8A1 to protect CH-47 and Huey helicopters. Once assembled, each revetment was filled with sand. They helped protect the choppers from mortar rounds.

Company D also built a 75 ft by 202 ft hanger towards the end of the project. This was interesting because all the parts were metric and our tools were english measurement. To make it more interesting, the instructions on assembling the hanger were in Japanese! Oh well, the guys just built it anyway. Engineer perseverance. Unfortunately, typhoon Frieda

came through in November and blew the roof off! I watched it simply lift off and float away. However, many of the metal sections were reusable and soon things were back to normal.

All the way through the many months of this project, guys, another job damn well done. Thank you.

Hanoi Hannah

Hanoi Hannah was an English speaking North Vietnamese radio propagandist. Her job was to tell us how bad things were going for the U.S.. On Fridays she would list the names of that week's U.S. dead. Her intelligence network was fantastic. She even announced the name and weight of the newborn child of a serviceman in Thailand - before he even knew!

But, she did play good music, and jazz late at night. I used to listen to her while at Phu Hiep. Imagine my astonishment when I heard the following late one night, *"This song is dedicated to Captain Richard F. Hill and the men of Company D of the 577th Engineer Battalion. Enjoy it, because you won't be there in there morning."* This really happened! I will never forget those words.

It took me a moment to come out of shock, and then to put the entire battalion on full alert. We manned the perimeter, and sure enough, within a short time the shooting started. It seemed to be about a platoon sized probe probably looking for weaknesses in our perimeter so that sappers could get in to destroy aircraft.

With everyone on the perimeter the attack slowed, though one enemy soldier got up to the wire and hid behind a few sandbags. Unfortunately for him, the sandbags were a support for a million candlepower flare that someone had scrounged and put outside the wire. I don't know who set it off, but a hundred yards of the line lit up instantly and so did our visitor.

While all this was to on, Spooky (aka Puff) was flying above dropping the same type flares over a total of five firefights spread all over the province. He seemed to have just enough time to get from one location to another just as that flare was dying out. Those guys were amazing and I'd see an even more impressive demonstration of their ability within a couple of months.

The Barber Who Was A Spy

The company had hired a Vietnamese barber to keep us from being too shaggy. He had a little one-man shop in a corner of the company area. He gave a good haircut, but it always bothered me to have my hair cut with a razor. I couldn't help but think that he might be a Viet Cong. But he did give a great scalp massage when he finished a cut.

And, no, he was not a Viet Cong. He was a North Vietnamese intelligence officer. He lost his job one day when the Vietnamese White Mice came and took him away. I still wonder what kind of intelligence he was gathering. The only thing we ever did in secret was a run to or from a special forces camp and only a very few people knew of those in advance. Maybe he just found a nice safe job, for a while.

QL-1

This was the only north-south highway in Vietnam. It ran from Hanoi to Saigon. It was one of the few paved roads (mostly) in either country. Bernard Fall referred to part of it as "The Street Without Joy" in his book of the same name, written about the French misadventures against the Viet Minh. As an aside, the Viet Minh commanding general was Vo Nguyen Giap, who also commanded the NVA and Viet Cong against the U.S.

Anyway, Company D, and all the others had tasks along this vital highway. Company B took care of maintenance down in the mountains near Vung Ro Bay. At this time, Company D was responsible for the highway from the northern base of the mountains all the way to Tuy Hoa, distance of about 25 kilometers. Some of the road was usable by military vehicles, but where it had been built through the rice paddies, it was a bear.

When the road had originally been constructed in that area, it was "floated." After many centuries of growing rice, the wet clay earth went down hundreds of feet before one came to anything solid. Put rock on such a surface and it disappeared. So, whomever originally built this super highway had perhaps used a thick layer of rice straw beneath sand and gravel, which was later paved to a width of perhaps 12 feet.

The problem faced on the paddy area of the road was that when a pothole developed that went down any depth, you could dump many cubic yards of rock into it with no progress. Company A busted their tails in several quarry operations to provide us with rock, and we just poured it into the earth!

Well, finally, a light went off and, for the large holes, we put rice straw in first, then rock, and then the asphalt platoon would patch it up.

MAJ Guba used to jump all over the drivers of any jeeps or ¾ ton trucks he saw go by a pothole with water in it. All vehicles had a shovel, and you had darn well better use it. Oh yes, make sure the hole is square against traffic! Of course, this was sorta fruitless in the monsoon season. During the previous monsoon Company B had recorded 114 inches of rain in 3 months.

Pipelines

The second platoon of the 643rd Engineer Company (Pipeline) was attached to Company D to build two pipelines, a 6 and an 8 inch diameter, to provide gasoline, diesel and JP4 jet fuel from a pump station at Port Lane, Vung Ro Bay to the base camp area and Tuy Hoa Air Force Base. The latter was home to an F-100 squadron that dropped bombs on Charlie and the NVA whenever they could.

The pipelines were made of steel tubes with Victaulic couplings. It was very easy to connect them together simply with two C-shaped couplings that bolted together. The pump station at Port Lane controlled the flow in each pipeline. Company B built the pump station.

The pipeline construction was pretty straightforward because the pipes were laid on top of the ground. We had intended to suspend it over the Song Van River that was about 100 ft wide with rather high banks, but the Logistics Command POL people in Saigon insisted that it be put underwater because the Viet Cong would blow it if suspended. I told them that Sir Charles was gonna blow it anyway and it would be fixed much faster if suspended.

Manhandling part of the larger pipeline at the river

Well, the rank was in Saigon, so we sent divers down to make a contour of the bottom.

Of course, the Viet Cong did blow the pipelines and did it underwater. I think they were repaired and replaced there three times. After that, we just suspended both pipelines above the water and didn't tell anyone.

And, strangely, while the pipelines were frequently opened and burnt, or blown elsewhere, they were never hit at the river again.

On the day that the picture above was taken, there was a pile of pipe just out of site to the left of the guys. One young man managed to get some of the pipes rolling off the stack, which in turn, severed a finger. Despite the amputation, it was not a serious injury. But, I called a Dustoff because the walk and drive to the hospital was about 13 kilometers. The Huey arrived a short time later and landed on the levee. I decided to ride back with him.

Now, most helicopter pilots have a rule that goes like "100 feet and 100 knots, or 1500 feet and as slow as you wish." Well, this pilot decided that flying over the rice paddies and 10 feet and over 100 knots was safer, so he did just that. Maybe lower.

Halfway back, I turned to check the patient and he was as white as a sheet. I asked if he was in pain. He couldn't talk, but indicated that his finger was fine. It was obviously his first helicopter flight and here he was about to crash, which was the only reason we could possibly be in such a precarious position. By the time we landed at the 91st he had calmed down a bit, realizing he was going to live.

And, with what should have been simply a few days recovery, as I wrote and assured his father, things became more serious. Infection set in. The hospital would send patients to Japan if they were there more than 3 weeks. And, as the deadline approached, the finger got better and his release was scheduled. Then it got infected again so they kept him for a bit longer, and then it got better. The poor guy was in the hospital for almost 2 months for a sore finger, but finally returned to duty. Just shows how easily injuries and wounds got infected in that part of the world.

I was out there a couple of times at night with the 643rd guys, the first time with a squad of infantry from the Sub-Area Command who were to provide security. Found them snoozing with the smell of pot in the air. We never again asked for their help.

One night, very late, the team of about a dozen men had to get out to QL-1 to the vehicles, but also had to go by a suspected Viet Cong village (Phu-Khe 2). All weapons were on full automatic, alternating pointing out left and right. The order was that if anything happen we wouldn't worry about where it came from, just rip off a full magazine and run. We got by the village, but then, right on the trail was a little man and his 50 or so ducks. All sound asleep. I passed the word to fire into the air and run like hell as soon as the ducks alerted.

Well, that man got the surprise of his life when the first duck quacked. Fourth of July. And, zoom, we were out to the road and on the way home.

Unfortunately, the pipeline platoon had some really nut types in it. The first real problem happened when a young man jumped out of a truck and a derringer type pistol fell out his pocket, hit the ground, went off and killed a 16 year old Vietnamese worker. More charges for the JAG types. And I had to officially pay the family a death gratuity, which was really very little, but not for them.

While waiting for the parents to return to their hut, a young boy stole the shovel right off my jeep, and neither I nor the driver saw it. He buried it in the sand by the jeep to be retrieved later. However, the Vietnamese Lieutenant in the back seat of the jeep, who was along as an interpreter, saw what happened and chased the boy behind the hut where he began to beat the crap out of him. I'm quite sure the officer did not care one bit about the shovel, but he had lost face by it happening with us in the jeep. I stopped him, of course, but once again, that pervasive mentality of so many of the people.

The day after the parents were paid, a young boy showed up wanting a job. Turns out he was the 14 year old brother of the victim. We could not hire anyone younger than 16 and it amazed me that the parents would even think of his working for us. He came back again the next day with someone who swore the kid was 16. Mentality again.

The next thing that happened occurred about 2200 one evening while I was working in the CP. The pipeline platoon leader dragged in a soldier

64

by the collar. The lieutenant was so upset he couldn't speak, but after he calmed down, he explained that he'd been on his cot asleep when the kid came in with a hand grenade in his hand and seemingly afraid. The pin was out, but handle was still on as he held it. The platoon leader started to get up, telling the boy to hold it tight. When he was halfway up, the kid dropped the grenade in the lieutenant's lap. As the handle flew off, the lieutenant shoved the guy out of the way and dove out of the tent and onto the grenade.

As he lay there on top of the grenade, it didn't go off and the rest of the platoon, who were all watching, roared with laughter. For some reason, it wasn't funny to the lieutenant.

In the CP, I reached for the "Red Book," the Uniform Code of Military Justice, and read a section to the guy. I asked if he understood it. No, so I read it again, and yet again. Finally, he said, "Yeh, I understand that I'm going to jail, right?"

Right. The charge was assault with a deadly weapon, cuz it didn't matter that the grenade had no detonator in it. The platoon leader didn't know that. Off to the jail at Long Binh.

All the negative things about the pipeline platoon were provably due to the fact that they had been separated from their parent company for a long time and had gotten a bit too independent.

More Civilian Deaths

Just a few days after the shooting death mentioned previously, one of our dump trucks was driving down QL-1 when a boy on a bicycle heavily overloaded with rice straw swerved right in front of the truck and was killed.

Then, days after that, a Vietnamese man was seemingly watching a crew repair QL-1. One of our trucks was about to dump a load of gravel. There was a safety man behind and beside the truck as required, but suddenly the man walked right behind the truck as the gravel came out. He was crushed and died at the scene.

A couple of days later I got a letter of reprimand from LTC Rodolph because of the 3 civilian deaths. I was pretty upset because two of them were obviously not our fault. But, as the saying goes, "The commander is responsible for everything his unit does, or does not, do."

I went to battalion headquarters to object to the C.O., but he wasn't there. I was talking to the adjutant about it and he said, "What letter? If there was any such letter, I would have been told to prepare and file it. Go away."

Well, the Boss was meeting his legal obligation to discipline me, but obviously didn't want to hurt my career. But, if asked, he could always say he sent the letter to me. Needless to say, I was relieved just a wee bit.

Flying Backwards

Again, for some long lost reason, I had to go down to the 18th Engineer Brigade headquarters at Dong Ba Thin. Another officer was with me, though I don't remember who. We got a ride down on a chopper and did whatever we had to do there. But we had no ride back, so we went to the airfield and started asking around.

There was a new O-1 Bird Dog FAC unit that had just arrived in-country and were getting themselves organized. I found the C.O., a major, and asked if they had any birds going north. He said that he and another pilot were making a training run to Qui Nhon. So I asked if the two of us could hook a ride in the back seats as far as Phu Hiep. He said he'd like to but they couldn't do it because they didn't have their emergency radios yet.

Well, I didn't see how they could go themselves without the radios, but I asked him if I could get two radios, could we go along? He said yes, and must have thought I was nuts.

Nutso walked over to the adjacent FAC unit and found the supply sergeant who said we could borrow two radios if he had a hand-receipt for them. Ok, so I put the major's name on the receipts and we started walking back to the flight line office, radios in hand.

As we got near the other unit there was a great WHOOSH and a rocket soared up and out across Cam Rahn Bay and hit an open field in the 22d Replacement Depot. The Sergeant in charge of the man loading the rocket on the plane screamed, "You idiot, I told you to leave that safety pin in there!" The young soldier had a rather badly burned hand but his sergeant wasn't cutting any slack.

The Bird Dog was equipped with two 2.75" "Willie Peter" white phosphorus rockets, the pilot could mark the target with a rocket that produced a large amount of smoke. The young troop now understood how that worked I'm sure.

Finally, we walked in the office and gave the radios to the major, who was rather incredulous to see them. The two planes took off a short time later.

We flew up the coast following QL-1 until we got to the mountains southwest of Vung Ro Bay. These were about 700 meters high and had some really strong winds. I was looking down at the ground when I realized we were going backwards! I never knew you could fly backwards, but we sure did. The pilot kinda thought it funny, even though dangerous, but finally turned around and went out to sea to avoid the mountains and the wind. A short time later we landed at Phu Hiep AAF.

The things that happen…

Prison Minefield

During the summer, July I think, I had a visitor to Company D. He was tall, black beard, black hat, black shirt, black jeans and black boots. He said he was from CORDS, a part of USAID, the U.S. Agency for International Development. CORDS was the Civil Operations and Revolutionary Development Support, a pacification program of the governments of South Vietnam and the United States. It was actually under the direct command of USARV, not USAID. Team 28 of CORDS was based in Tuy Hoa.

That story lasted about 15 seconds as he asked me if we could put in a minefield for a prison at Tuy Hoa North. In this war CORDS was frequently a cover for the CIA much of the time, and so it was here. I later found out he was part of Operation Phoenix as well, but more on that later.

I told him that minefields were the job of the combat engineers and we were construction engineers. He replied that we were the only engineers in the area and then repeated his question. I then told him we could do it if he cleared it with my commander.

This is where it begins to get interesting for, though he got clearance, there is absolutely no record of it, or of anything about a minefield being built in the battalion after action reports. Nor is there anything on Google.

Anyway, we went up to the province interrogation center. It was double-walled but on the North side, the outer wall had been destroyed. Spook told me that they had 1700 NVA prisoners in a facility built for 100, including many officers, and that the commander of the 95th NVA Regiment had sworn to release the prisoners. The spook expected the attack before, or during, the upcoming elections on 1 - 2 September.

On the way back to our base camp, I passed the gate to the city of Tuy Hoa. There were 3 human heads impaled there. I don't know for sure, but I was told that they were put there by the ROK infantry as a message to the Viet Cong. Or maybe by Phoenix. Or maybe by the Viet Cong. Turned my stomach, no matter who did it.

I returned to the CP and determined that we would install M24 "Bouncing Betty" mines every 6 feet in the open area. This is an anti-personnel mine designed so that, when tripped, a small propelling charge launches the body of the mine 3-4 feet into the air, where the main charge detonates and sprays fragmentation at roughly waist height. Each M24 would be ringed by four M14 "Toe Popper" plastic mines, designed to ruin a foot. This combination would be lethal.

The mines were ordered (construction engineers don't keep such toys lying around). Then I asked my hot shots if they would volunteer to install the mines. These were guys who had repeatedly asked to be transferred to a helicopter door gunner MOS, which I always refused to do. Of course, they all volunteered. The best of the best.

As an aside, on a lovely evening around 2008, one of these guys called me at home in Alachua, FL, and just said he wanted to thank me for not granting the transfer because he was sure it had saved his life. That was one of the proudest days of my life and I don't mind admitting that the tears flowed.

When we began installing the mines, I saw that many prisoners were watching from the inner wall! What the hell? I asked the Vietnamese prison commander to get them down where they could not take note of the minefield layout. He said he could not do that because he only had 21 guards to watch 1700 prisoners on a 24/7 basis. And he was afraid to try it.

I asked who the leader was and he pointed him out. I said, "Okay, get him down here." This was a stupid decision that was definitely in violation of tons of rules of war, but a 27 year old Captain is allowed one mistake. Uh, one more mistake.

I gestured for the man to carry the full boxes of mines from the truck to a stack near the work. Then I turned my attention to the installation. We had no minefield record forms, of course, so I was using graph paper to make a record of the field.

When I looked back at the POW, he was still at work, but laying the boxes out in a line heading right for a box of fuses. Duh, did he really think he could arm one of the mines and do something with it? Guess so, but that didn't seem so great to me. I went to my jeep, picked up a shotgun and tapped him on the shoulder and when he turned, put the gun in his face and gestured back towards the main pile of mines. He got the message and stacked everything nicely.

After the field was complete, I duplicated the layout record and gave a copy to Mr. Spook, to be used if the mines had to be removed. The other copy was sent up the chain of command to whomever kept such things.

After the elections in September, I saw him again and he told me that the prison had been attacked and that the mines had done their job, killing and injuring many attackers.

Operation Phoenix? This was a CIA operation that ran from 1967 until 1971. The mission was to assassinate the infrastructure of the Viet Cong operating from local villages. It was a joint U.S.-Vietnamese operation. I have a dear friend who was assigned to such a team as a SP-4. To this day he carries the horrific memories of what his team did to so many people. He had been attending medical school and got drafted over a summer break. The experience was so terrible that he later became a psychiatrist at the VA Hospital in West Palm Beach who specialized in PTSD. He treated only Vietnam Vets, including me.

Also regarding Operation Phoenix, around 2006 I was doing some research online and looked it up. A few days later I got a phone call from someone who refused to identify himself, and who was demanding to know how I heard about Operation Phoenix, which he insisted never existed.

Well, that took a bit of thinking about, and I finally said that if it never existed then it didn't matter what I thought about it, and then I hung up. Never have figured that one out, but somebody was doing some online monitoring way back then.

ROK Ambulance

Late one evening I had gone down to the motor pool and was chatting with Clovis Steelman. Things had been quiet for several weeks so the area was quite lit up for the night shift's work. As we spoke, I saw an ambulance drive into the motor pool and stop near some boxed tools. This was strange because the battalion had no ambulances.

Then the back door opened and out came several ROK marines who started picking up the boxes. Both Clovis and I yelled at them but they just waved and continued tossing boxes into the vehicle. We both started running at them and as I ran by my jeep I grabbed my M-16.

The ambulance pulled out of the motor pool and took off for the gate to the QL-1 access road. They weren't gonna stop, so I took aim and ripped off most of a 20-round magazine. That didn't stop them and I don't know if I hit the vehicle. We never heard anything more and even though we knew they'd drive right to the ROK compound, it didn't make sense to chase them. The Koreans were a tough bunch and didn't like us at all.

Cam Rahn Bay

Cam Rahn Bay had an enormous supply depot. It was so large that the folks who ran it often didn't know everything that was in it. This made problems for the battalion because when we had something to build we couldn't follow the normal process. Instead of designing the work, ordering what we needed and then getting to work — well, it just didn't flow like that in 'Nam. More often than not, we'd get a project, find out what materials were available and then design around what was there. Sometimes awkward, but it worked.

To expedite things the battalion kept a warrant office and a lieutenant at Cam Ranh. Their job was to get what we needed from the depot. It worked like this: Requisitions would go to this team, they would ask the depot to fill them, and quite often the requisitions came back saying the materials were not there and needed to be backordered.

Our guys knew better. After convincing the depot people that they really were not there to steal things, the dynamic duo was allowed to roam the depot at will. And, when a requisition came back, they were often able to tell the depot staff exactly where the materials asked for were located. At other times they found substitute materials.

All this wasn't because of incompetence in the depot, but simply because supplies were coming in faster than they could be properly accounted for. Thus the reason for the dynamic duo.

Sometime during my stint with Company D, I had reason to go to Cam Ranh Bay. Again, I have no idea why, but orders be orders. So, off we go in my tired jeep. I should point out that the drive down that 120 or so miles is quite lovely, other than encounters with the occasional Viet Cong. But this trip was quiet and we were able to enjoy the mountains and the beautiful beaches of Nha Trang, which QL-1 runs right beside. It seemed strange to see bikini clad young ladies sunning themselves, playing games and swimming. For some reason, my driver ran off the road while staring at these beauties. I, of course, was not looking at them.

Kool-Aid Kid

Not long after the motor pool fiasco, it was time for CW2 Clovis W. Steelman to rotate home. It's nice to remember that his wife wrote to him twice on every single day he was in-country. And in each letter she enclosed a pack of Kool-Aid, since she had read that GI's liked the stuff.

Now that is a really nice story, except for the fact that Clovis absolutely hated Kool-Aid, and even if he liked it, we always had it available in the mess hall. But, because his wife had gone to all that trouble, and because he felt that he couldn't tell her the truth, he'd kept every single pack she'd sent, some 700 plus! They were all in a footlocker and when he left us, he turned the box over to the mess sergeant.

Just before rotating home, Clovis had one more trip down to Cam Rahn Bay with a re-supply convoy. After loading up, they spent the night there and the next morning were first in line awaiting the gate to QL-1 to be opened. He was in the lead vehicle, a ¾ ton truck, and he was very nervous for some reason. Just before the gate opened a Korean ¾ ton pulled up beside him and Clovis waved him on. The convoy followed a few minutes later. Less than a mile down the road they came on the ROK truck, totally destroyed by a mine with all in it dead. Steelman's intuition had saved his life.

It was very common for those about to go home to get very anxious as their DEROS approached. For some it was a month or more early, but for most it seemed to be at about 2 weeks. From that time until they departed, they avoided anything dangerous, even seemingly routine things as well. Most commanders recognized this and tried to accommodate the problem.

Some men, however, pushed past that fear and kept going. It seemed that these were the ones who died at the very end of their tour of duty. I knew several.

I've not been able to locate Clovis Steelman, but I want the world to know that he is one of the finest human beings I have ever met. Maybe we can have a glass of Kool-Aid someday, if he ever learned to like it.

Wanted - Captain Ken Jobe

In the late spring, Ken Jobe was still the C.O. of Company B at Vung Ro Bay. Each Friday he would drive up to the battalion base camp for a staff meeting, and then return in the evening around sundown. One day he noticed some different looking woodcutters on the mountain. We talked it over and decided that, given the lateness of the hour, the likelihood the ROK's had closed/barricaded QL-1 for the night and that Ken and his jeep driver would be out gunned should an event occur, it would be best to find a bunk for the night at base camp. Seemed wise as he had a 10,000 piaster reward on his head.

The location was the site of an NVA/VC ambush that same evening which took out a transportation company jeep with a SSG and his driver.

Never did figure out why Ken was worth so much money. 10,000 P was about $50 USD at the time. Nobody ever put a bounty on my sorry butt. I'm jealous.

IG Inspection

Around late May or early June the 577th had its first in-country Inspector General inspection. I wasn't worried about it, but I did get orders to prepare for the inspection. It seems that each battalion was allowed one dog as a pet. There were 28 dogs in our base camp area. The Boss told me to get rid of them for the inspection, so they were loaded up and taken to Company B at Vung Ro Bay.

Our paperwork, the thing that these REMFS usually get incensed over, was good. But the Colonel who was in charge really crawled me for having loaded weapons, of all things, lying around all over the company area! I tried to remind him that we *were* in a combat zone, but he didn't think that was good enough. He told me I needed to secure the weapons until needed.

I looked at him for a moment and then said, "You mean like Company A across the street did, lock them up in a CONEX container?" He said, "Yes." I said, "No, not until my C.O. orders me to and maybe not then." Boy was he pissed. But what was he gonna do, send me to Vietnam?

Larry Gralla redistributed his weapons to his men when the inspection team left for Company B the next day. And, that same morning, our doggie truck returned from there. Unfortunately, it was stopped at the ROK roadblock and the driver was questioned as to his destination. When he got back, there were no dogs in the truck. Goddam Korean dog eaters!

Bailey Bridge Blown

On 15 July the double single Bailey Bridge over the Song Cua River just north of and at the base of the mountain at Vung Ro Bay was blown up. It had been built by Company B earlier in the year and was supposedly protected by the ROK marine company which had a camp about 2 km

north on QL-1. In the picture, a Huey in the upper left is seen bringing in VIP "after the fact" folks, and a train can just be seen in the lower left middle of the picture. That train was subsequently blown up by a 250 lb bomb on election day as it moved on up the tracks to repair a railroad bridge beside the pipeline river crossing. The bridge itself had been blown before my time.

There were also some caves in the area sometime used by the Viet Cong. CPT Jobe and about 5 men started exploring those caves the morning the bridge was blown until his maintenance warrant officer persuaded him to stop. He was following VC foot prints in the soft limey silt. That WO was an excellent hunter and decided there were considerably more of them than the five engineers. So, discretion being the better part of valor, the group went back to the construction business.

About four hours later COL Bullmoose, I mean Hospelhorn, who was the Sub-Area Commander, showed up with a god awful quad.50 and proceeded to waste mucho ammo firing into the hill. Jobe had his guys take cover because the spent casings and the ricochets were dangerous.

This bridge would soon be seen again, with similar woes to come.

Cannibals

The cannibals I speak of were mechanics and they were all over the place even though cannibalization of parts from deadlined vehicles was against regulations, sometimes it had to be done to keep things running.

In 1967 there were five echelons (levels) of maintenance, which were:

(1) First echelon maintenance was performed by the equipment operator. This was routine fluid checks, air pressures, etc.

(2) Second echelon maintenance was that done by the organization, in this case the line companies B, C and D. This included tire replacement, oil changes, painting and a lot that they were not supposed to do, but did well.

(3) Third echelon maintenance was that done by Company A, which had a great capability to fix most anything that broke.

(4) Fourth echelon maintenance was that done by units organized as semi-fixed or permanent shops to serve lower echelons within a geographic area. For us, this was Cam Rahn Bay.

(5) Fifth echelon maintenance was depot level authorized for overhauling major items, assemblies, parts, accessories, tools, and test equipment, and normally supplied on an overhaul-and-return-to-stock basis. This was normally Japan or the U.S..

What all this gobbledygook means is that if A company couldn't fix it, we usually didn't see it again and had to order a new piece of equipment, which could take some time. And, when something left Company A it was often shipped out on an LST (Landing Ship Tank) or a RORO (Roll On - Roll Off) ship. This was because that was the easiest way to load and unload heavy equipment. The small stuff, like spares for jeeps, we usually had, traded for, or ~~stole~~.

Back to the big stuff. Knowing we were going to be needing parts for other heavy equipment, when something went to a ship, so did the mechanics, at least this is what I heard later, because you know that a company commander could not allow something that was against regulations, right?

Anyway, the dozer or scraper, whatever, being shipped out usually was much lighter when the ship departed. And the mechanics came back with truckloads of cannibalized parts, all done to make sure our mission got accomplished.

Chapter 3 - Dong Tre (Aug)

On 28 June Company C was deployed to Dong Tre special forces camp to construct an all weather 2,800 foot runway with crossovers and parking apron for a C-123 airstrip and to perform road maintenance. The runway, apron and taxiways were to be brought to grade with 44,000 cubic yards of fill material, and then sealed with asphalt. M8A1 plank were to be used for the finished surface. Company C also had the mission to upgrade 13 kilometers of Route TL-2D to carry class 35 traffic and to maintain 18 kilometers of route TL-6B which connected between TL-2D and QL-1 north of Tuy Hoa. These routes comprised the only land access route to Dong Tre from QL-1.

Special Forces Team A-222 was located at Dong Tre in the central portion of II Corps Tactical Zone in the middle of the hilly Ha Boung River Valley, inland from the coast. Team A-222 conducted saturation patrolling throughout this valuable rice-producing region and also guarded the district capital of Le Hai.

Company C's C.O. and I had previously flown to Dong Tre to recon the jobs. We studied the area for the runway, which was a semi-dry rice paddy. We also discussed the possible bivouac areas. At first, it had not been determined which company, C or D, would be sent. It was decided to send Company C to give them experience in building this type of airfield.

Mortar Lightning

Dan Bell tells the story about mortar lightning, or was it lightning mortar?

One cold and stormy night in Dong Tre it was full of lightning and thunder. Rain was coming down in buckets when suddenly a bolt of lightning came out of the sky and hit a stack of asphalt drums which exploded and caused a fire ball a hundred feet in the air. An alert was called and everyone came out of their tents and jumped into the bunkers with all their web gear and rifles. I was on guard at the front gate with a guy named Chavez and we both saw the lightning bolt hit. LT Betz came running out and asked us what happened and we told him. He said NO that was a mortar. Pissed me off... He called me a liar. And all those guys had to sit in the cold and mud all night because of that LT.

First Death

On July 5th PFC Donald E. Heinz of Company C was killed in a vehicle accident. He was the first soldier from the 577th to die in the Vietnam War.

Mortar Attack

Keith Treesh joined the 577th on 11 March 1967 and drove a 5 ton dump truck. He was first in Company D later transferred to Company C when they went to Dong Tre. Keith was wounded in a mortar attack in July and was flown out back to the 91st Hospital in Tuy Hoa to recover from his wounds.

Reassigned

In late July, I was awaiting assignment to relinquish command of Company D, become a staff officer and maybe get more sleep. It was USARV policy that a company commander would only command for 6 months, due to the hours and strain involved. I'd been in command for over 6-½ months. Little did I know…

On the morning of 30 July I was told to come to battalion headquarters on the double. Once there, I was "asked" by LTC Rodolph if I would "like" to take command of Company C. There was only one answer, of course. He said I would take command as soon as I could get there and a helicopter would pick me up in 20 minutes. I ran back to D Co. orderly room, hollered at the First Sergeant that I was leaving and to tell Lieutenant Doug Booth that he was taking command of Company D immediately. I grabbed my gear and headed for the heliport.

The reason for all this was that there had been a murder in Company C, over a beer can opener, the night before. The former C.O. had been relieved of command and was to become the battalion S-4 (supply) officer. I flew to Dong Tre where I got out of the helicopter on one side as the he got in the other. Formal change of command, Vietnam style.

I am sure that CPT Richardson had done his very best, but what with his company having the first two deaths in the battalion in the one year it had been in-country, and neither by enemy action, it was just too much to overlook. The army dictates that, "The commander is responsible for everything his unit does, and does not do." And that includes things that may not be within his control at all. It seems harsh, but it has generally worked for as long as our country has been going to war.

First Impressions

There was a lot of disorganization in the company and they didn't have all the weapons they were supposed to, much less adequate ammunition. It was not good.

I was not the least impressed with the First Sergeant. He, as with some other NCO's, had been recalled from retirement for a two year period. As an enticement, a promotion of one grade was given. Perhaps a good idea to fill the NCO ranks of new units, but, for example, promoting a retired E-5 SGT to E-6 SSG seemed odd. If you couldn't make E-6 in 20 years there had to be a reason that was not good. The 1SGT filled this bill.

To me, the company's top NCO sounded like he was straight out of the army of the 1920s. Whenever he spoke to me it was, "Does the Captain want…" or "Does the Captain wish to…" or "Would the Captain like… This form of address was archaic and it drove me nuts! At first I wasn't sure if he was trying to impress me, or if he was just dumb. It didn't take long to come to a conclusion. I finally had to tell him he had 3 choices. He could call me just plain "Captain," "Captain Hill," or "Sir." Nothing else.

For some unknown reason, the unit had built a prefabricated plywood orderly room/command post, which was shipped to Vietnam in pieces from the U.S., trucked to Phu Hiep, and then to Dong Tre, where it was assembled. I thought that was what tents were for! But, it was already there, so it would stay, being the only thing left behind when we departed.

Shortly after arriving, I asked the First Sergeant to take me on a tour of the company's defenses. The camp was located on the lower slope of Hill 142, which was quite steep. We walked behind the CP and I began climbing the hill, stopping every 20 feet up the hill. Then I would pick up a rock and bounce it off the CP. We continued doing this until I could not throw a rock within 50 feet of the building. Finally, the First Sergeant asked what I was doing. I pointed out that the existing "perimeter" wire was one roll of concertina barbed wire almost laying against the CP. "But, what is the Captain doing?" Throwing hand grenades, I replied. He didn't get it. And he was still talking stupid.

Operations

Overall, the location of the bivouac wasn't good, but there was little choice. There was no room in the SF camp and the valley was rice paddy. Having high ground above us was bad, but it being quite a steep hill was good, and we put a manned radio relay station at the top. It would be pretty difficult for the Viet Cong to get to us from there.

There were several really good NCO's in the company and due to them, we were able to make many security and other changes in a very short time.

The new perimeter wire, a triple roll concertina, was put all around the camp, always at least 50 feet from anything. We installed claymore mines in concrete outside the wire, so the enemy could not turn them back on us. And we obtained the missing machine guns, grenade launchers and ammunition. All this took a few days, by which time the tents were sandbagged and a bunker started.

We had to halt construction work in order to prepare the company for even a minor attack. Apparently, the leadership hadn't really considered that the unit could be in grave danger. Perhaps being adjacent to a special forces camp, with 13 Americans and 50+ Vietnam Civilian Irregular Defense Group soldiers (CIDG) gave a false sense of security, but the 95th NVA Regiment had the area pretty much surrounded.

Nearly Fatal Demonstration

Few in the company had seen a claymore mine work, so I had some cardboard boxes put about 100 meters from a mine at the airfield site. The detonating wire was fed back 50 meters behind the mine to a ditch where the trigger was attached and cover from the backblast was available. The mine was set off with a big blast and shredded boxes.

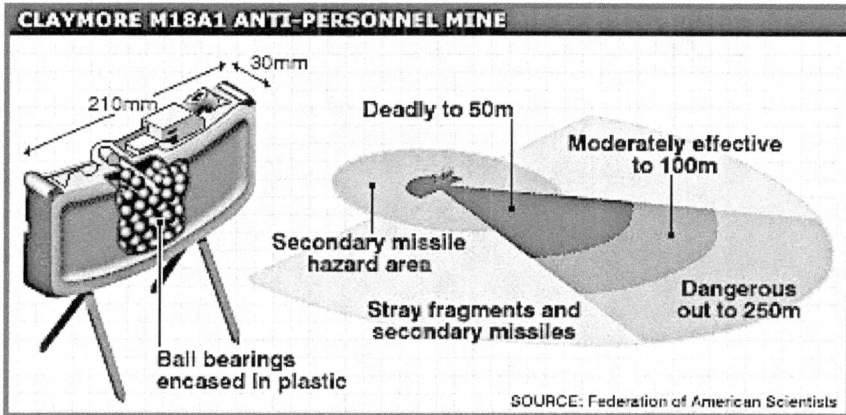

CLAYMORE M18A1 ANTI-PERSONNEL MINE

30mm

210mm

Deadly to 50m

Moderately effective to 100m

Secondary missile hazard area

Dangerous out to 250m

Stray fragments and secondary missiles

Ball bearings encased in plastic

SOURCE: Federation of American Scientists

Nice demonstration, except for one thing, and I had made a very big mistake. I, too, had assumed safety by being adjacent to the SF camp and in daylight.

Soon after the mine detonation, we were taken under fire by a AK47. I could hear the gun and the bullets going overhead, but couldn't see the shooter. I ordered everyone down and, for those with weapons, directed fire adjacent to the village at the edge of the jungle, east of the runway. Right direction or not, the firing quickly stopped and we returned to our perimeter on the double!

This was a lesson I would never need to learn again. Fortunately, no one was injured.

Since the 2800 foot runway was being built in a "dry" rice paddy composed of clay, the amount of water in it had to be gotten out. That meant moving it around and aerating it. The graders did great job on this, but it seemed that we would never get the water content low enough. We tested the percentage water in the soil in a special can that held a small amount of dirt and sodium metal. The can was sealed and the moisture reacted with the sodium. Based on the pressure in the attached gauge, we knew what the water content was. Lots of testing, lots of aerating, but finally we would able to begin laying the M8A1 matting.

Soil moisture testing was a constant operation.

SSG James Allan was the Operations NCO and did an excellent co-ordinating all the daily equipment assignments and numerous other tasks that had to be done. Part of his work included estimating how much gravel fill would be needed for the airfield and finding the best place to get it. Scotty had a most interesting background.

He was born in Chicago but raised in Scotland, ironically passing through Ellis Island going the opposite direction! Scotty became a carpenter and cabinet maker in Scotland at age 14. He never knew that he was a U.S. citizen until WWII when young Scottish men were drafted in to the Scottish/British Regiments. Because he was U.S. citizen, he wasn't allowed to join his local regiment, The Cameronians (Scottish Rifles).

In either late 1943 or early 1944 he was taken to a U.S. unit in Northern England where he was inducted into the U.S. Army and taken to France while still in his Scottish street clothes, issued a uniform and weapons, and trained in the field. Shortly after he was on the move with the 1st Infantry Division when they crossed the Rhine at Remagen.

WWII ended soon thereafter, but he stayed in Germany with the Army of Occupation until 1950. He served as a guard to Nazi Rudolf Hess who ironically had crash landed in his home town in Hamilton Scotland. He participated in the Berlin Airlift, and also in breaking the Berlin Blockade. He ended up a Sergeant in the 11th Airborne in Italy before he was sent "home" to the U.S., where he hadn't been since he was an infant. He didn't serve in Korea because had just returned from overseas duty.

As a civilian between 1950 and 1963, he worked mostly as a carpenter. In 1963, now in his 30's, he joined the Army a second time. Since It had been many years since he left the Army, he had to start all over including basic training and loss of prior rank. He graduated basic training as a PFC with WWII awards and jump wings.

Quite a story about an outstanding NCO, most of which I was not aware of at Dong Tre. His son, Jim Allan filled out the details.

Mine Sweeps

While the runway construction was going on, the men conducted daily mine sweeps on Route TL-2D. This was another new task for these construction engineers, something normally done by trained combat en-

gineers. But, in Vietnam, engineers were engineers and this became just another job.

Each morning, a mine sweep team left the perimeter. The team included a squad for the sweep and one for security. This normally included one lead 5-ton dump truck which had been reinforced with ¾" steel plates in the cab flooring, with a layer of sandbags on top. The driver and shotgun also sat on spare flak jackets in addition to the ones they wore. The front fender wells had a framework of rebar welded in to contain additional sandbags to help absorb any blast received by the vehicle. The second truck was for transporting the security squad. In addition, my jeep, WETSU by name, provided additional security with an M60 machine gun mounted in the passenger area. The jeep also carried additional ammunition, frag and smoke grenades, C-4 plastic explosives and detonators.

The team didn't have to sweep through the village of Xuan Phuoc because we knew that Viet Cong lived there and they would not mine that part of the road. Interestingly, the village was the closest to the special forces camp. The picture below is the start of a sweep and with all the villagers around, there are obviously no mines around this part of the road. My driver is standing in my gun jeep with the M-60.

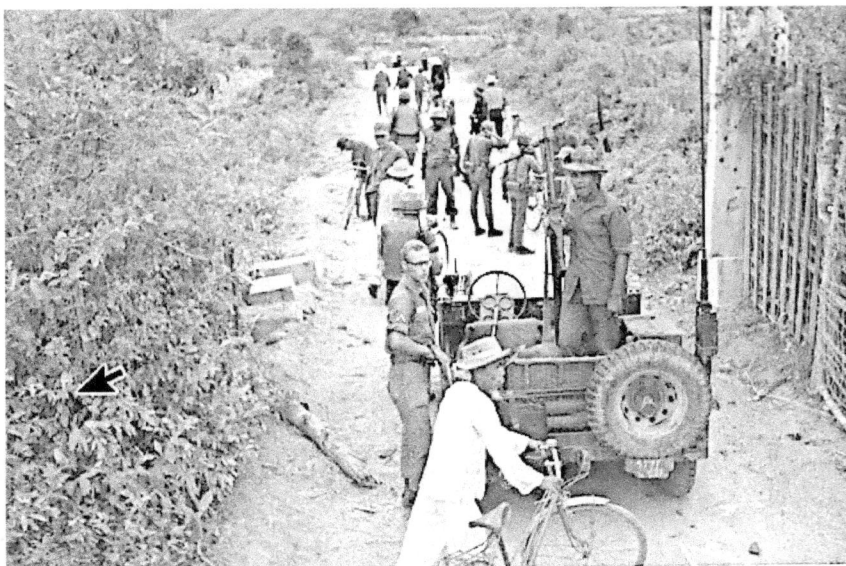

How did we know there were Viet Cong in that village? When Dad was in the boonies, the kids would come out to get candy from our men, but when Dad was home, there were no children to be seen. And maybe CPT John Seiver, the SF team leader might have told me that. This complex intelligence is great, eh?

Here is one of the CIDG troops with a .50 cal on the headache board of a 5-ton dump truck, ready to start a sweep.

The road that we had to upgrade, Route TL-2D, was really nothing more than a typical backwoods dirt road leading into the camp but it was the only way in. We widened it in places, installed and replaced culverts, etc. Certainly not a major project. But then there were those annoying mines that had to be found before work could be done - every day.

A large amount of gravel fill would be needed to stabilize the soil of the runway and also to upgrade the road. To do this, we opened a borrow pit about 2 ½ km north on 2D. After the sweep team passed, the scrapers and front loaders could safely get to the borrow pit and begin work.

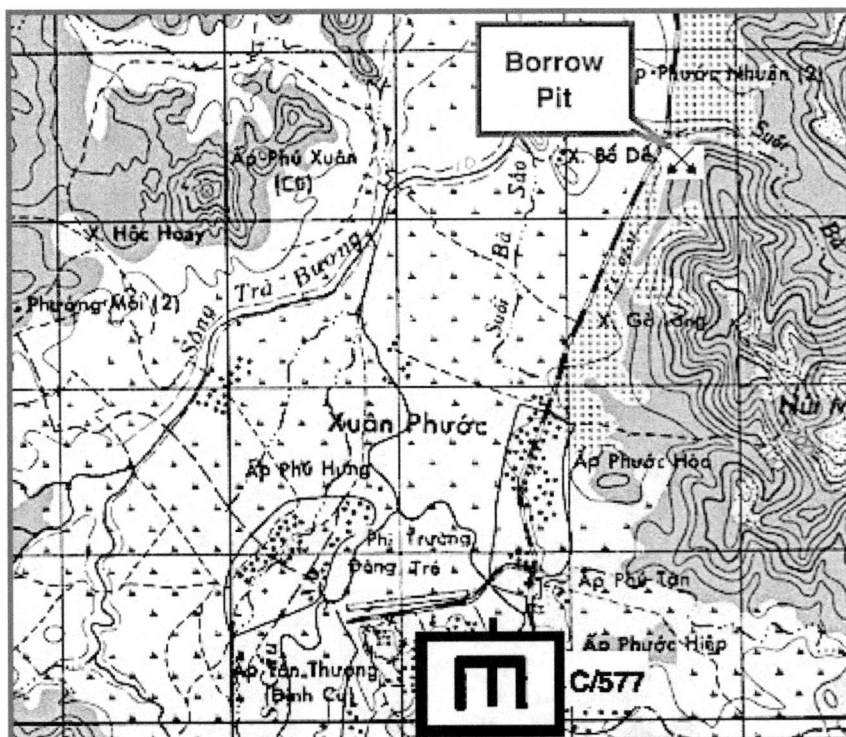

The sweep team would continue on up the road to route TL-6B, a total of about 10 km. The soldier on the mine detector had a harrowing and exacting job. If the mine detector was set with a high sensitivity hen he heard frequent mind bending screeches from every nail, bullet or shell casing he swept over. Set too low and he could miss a mine that might blow up under a vehicle wheel, or under his foot.

When a mine, usually homemade, was found, it was detonated with a charge of C-4. On one occasion, however, we found a stock of about fifty "butterfly bombs", BLU-3 cluster submunitions. It looked as though the larger bomb canister the contained the clusters had failed to open and arm the weapons. Or, they may have just not exploded when hitting the ground. In and case, they had been collected by the VC, who certainly knew what they were. We were not going to play with them. We called

the artillery battery temporarily located near our camp, who sent out an M42 twin 40mm "Duster."

The Duster crew had a ball when I told them to "Shoot 'em up!"

One evening after the scrapers had come in for the day, I noticed on operator marking the side of his tires with chalk. Curious, I asked what he was doing. To my surprise he said, "Marking the bullet hits, sir."

What?

Turns out that Charlie was taking pot shots at the pans as they worked on the road, trying perhaps to blow the tires and cause a wreck. Hey, those were really heavy duty tires and the bullets just bounced off! The operators, unfortunately, could not hear rifle fire over the noise, and thus didn't know they were shot at until the got off the rig. The Clark 290M was powered by a Cummins 380hp, 855 cubic inch, six cylinder diesel engine. Lotta noise!

More seriously, though, the crew at the borrow pit would take a few incoming rounds in the mornings, not too long after beginning work. These were more harassment than anything else, but it did interrupt work. I couldn't figure out why until I learned that the ROK Tiger Division was chasing the 95th NVA Regiment over in the next valley to the West. Apparently, some of their soldiers were exfiltrating at night and used a dry creek bed that ran right by the borrow pit. Sometimes they would not make it through at night and were somewhat in the open in the daytime. So the locals would pop off a few rounds at our crew, who would seek cover and then the NVA could sneak by.

One day, as the mine sweep team passed the pit, I had a machine gun team drop off and move up the steep hill just south of the pit area. They moved to the North side military crest and set up. When the shooting started they, and one of the platoon leaders returned fire from my jeep.

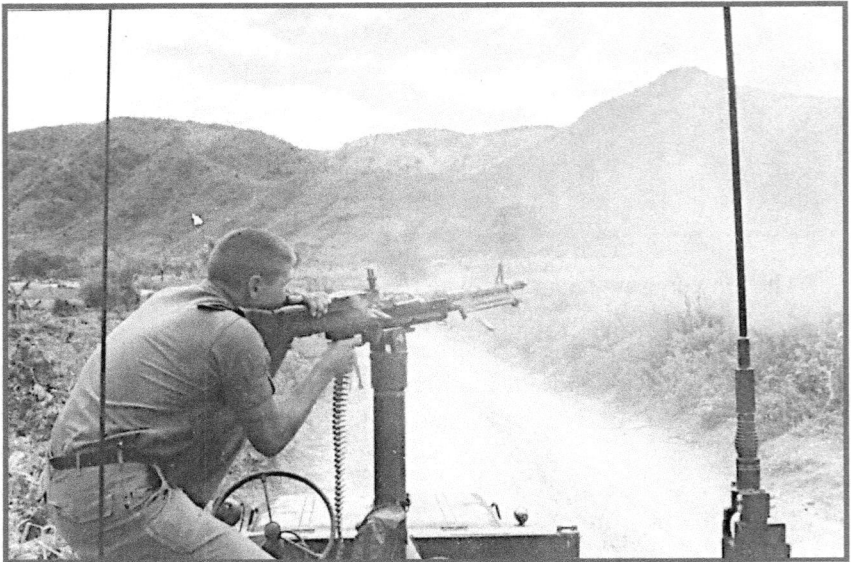

This time we continued to receive incoming fire and I could see where some of it was coming from but the gun team couldn't, so I decided to call in an artillery strike. I located the target coordinates and got on the radio to contact the SF team, but even though it was a short distance, I couldn't get through. So I radioed our commo people back on Hill 142 behind the bivouac. I gave them the fire mission data, they called the CP by wire phone, who called the A-Team, who gave it to a translator, who gave it to the CIDG gunners on their two 105mm howitzers. Whew!

The first round came in and hit the hilltop just behind the crest and our MG team. The top of the hill was in between the gun azimuth and the target. Scared the crap out of our guys but they were in no danger. Now I had the problem of trying to tell the howitzer guys to fire high angle and clear the hilltop. This led to some interesting conversations with all those steps in between me and the guns. But, finally, the word got through and the rounds fell on the target, though by that time Chuck would have split

A Battery of the 6/32 Artillery would come in about halfway through the month. Had they been there, the mission would have gone off flawlessly.

Near Disaster

On another day when the borrow pit was fired on rather heavily, I decided to send the men at the borrow pit to counterattack. I told the platoon leader, a second lieutenant, where I wanted him to go to advance on line and then lay down a base of fire. Then, since we now had an 8-inch howitzer battery within range, I was again going to call in artillery. I told the lieutenant to stop his advance at a specific spot and go no further to avoid casualties from friendly fire. Three times I told him, pointing the spot on the map and on the ground, and had him repeat my orders each time.

Off he and about 20 men went, while I contacted the FDC (fire direction center) at an 8-inch battery about 10 miles away. I gave them the target coordinates for the fire mission. The FDC controller told me they were firing another mission and would begin ours within a moment.

I looked up and saw my men actually on the target itself, and at that moment the FDC replied, "On the way, wait." That meant the initial round had been fired. It would take less than a minute to hit. I stood up and screamed as hard as I could to get the lieutenant's attention and to get his men out of danger.

I don't know what I said, but I do know it damaged my voice forever. And, thankfully, they heard me and took off running back towards us. Just a few moments later, the round hit exactly where it was intended to. The men had run fast enough to escape, barely.

Given a correct fire mission where the observer knows both his own location on the map and the location of the target, the first round fired by a U.S. 8-inch howitzer is accurate within 50 meters at a range of up to 16,800 meters. The round weighs 200 lbs and has a casualty radius of 50 meters. In other words, my troops would have been destroyed had they not run.

The picture below was taken by my driver.

My voice was so shot that I could hardly chew that young lieutenant's butt up one side and down the other, but of course I did just that. He was soon reassigned back to Headquarters Company in the battalion base camp where he couldn't hurt anyone.

Strafed By Brass

Incidents at the borrow pit continued to happen and I was getting fed up. So, again calling on the helicopter resources at Phu Hiep, I arranged a counter ambush that I hoped would end the problems by asking to have a gunship hang out beyond the mountains to our west until we called him in the next morning, but I didn't know just how the aviation folks would work this. And right on time, the guys at the pit were taking fire so I called the guns in. My driver and I were down on the ground on either side of the jeep when a Huey slick came dawdling in as a decoy. Sure enough, when he got over the pit, fairly heavy fire came at him. The slick pulled pitch and rose fast. Moments later the gunship roared in, opening fire first with 14 2.75 inch rockets and then with the mini-guns mounted on either side of the ship, followed by the automatic 40 mm grenade launcher in the nose.

Huey gunship in one of many configurations.

As he zoomed over our heads at about 50 feet, the thousands of brass cartridges from the mini-guns came down on us. I thought at first he'd fired the guns early and nearly missed us, but no, he was right on target. Still scared the bejesus out of the two of us.

It was one hell of a lot of firepower and it pretty much resolved the problem.

40 mm Boom

The day after a minor Viet Cong probe of our defenses, I was walking through the camp with SFC Allan when a soldier came up and said, "Sir, what do I do with this?"

In his hand was a round from an M-79 grenade launcher (Thumper) and it had been fired, meaning it was a dud. The M-79 round does not arm itself until it has traveled about 30 meters from the gun, but there is no way to tell if one has armed, or not, once fired. And it had a "kill radius" of 5 meters.

Needless to say, we all had to be careful. About 3 meters behind the trooper there was a large rock, so I told him to carefully walk to the rock and very gently place the grenade on the ground so I could blow it up afterwards. I asked if he understood and he said he did. Then he took one step and tossed the grenade which exploded as it hit the ground.

Lady Luck was with us that day because the grenade fell right behind the rock, which shielded everyone from the blast.

CIA Drops In

Just as we had roughed out the eastern runway overrun and begun on the runway, a very strange aircraft zoomed in and landed in less than 100 feet. Yes, less than 100 feet.

The pilot then climbed out and had a 20 minute visit with someone in the village adjacent to the airfield. Since this plane landed on a rough surface in as short a distance as it did, there was little doubt that the CIA had dropped in. I wondered how he planned to take off, and soon found out.

When the pilot returned, he cranked up the engine and then backed up... Yes, I said backed up, to the end of the overrun. He then revved the engine way up and took off in less than 100 feet at an extreme rate of climb, well over 30 degrees. Amazing!

I later found out that the aircraft type was a Pilatus PC-6 Porter, which were owned by Air America, a well known CIA cover.

One shot up bird dog

Not long after that visit, I got a radio message from the ROK battery requesting permission to land a plane. Since the runway was not nearly complete and we had equipment all over the place, I told them no way.

About ten minutes later, there is another request, same answer. Five minutes later, a panicky third request, but this time they tell me that the plane is a FAC O-1 Bird Dog that has been shot up and is almost out of fuel. Why didn't you tell me? Of course he can try to land!

We cleared the field as fast as possible and as the last equipment rolled off, the plane landed. I have never seen anything so shot up and still capable of flying. The pilot was wounded but okay. We pushed the plane off the field where it stayed until a truck picked it up.

In doing my research for this book, I learned that the ROK Tiger Division had, at that time, three O-1's. Two were painted olive drab and the third was unpainted aluminum. The one we saw was aluminum. The picture below is one of the others, which probably flew out of Qui Nhon.

The House Of Ill Repute

One fine day, three young ladies showed up on a motor scooter. They quickly built a "hooch" and opened for business.

I really didn't care if our horny young men visited the ladies — they would anyway! I had earlier made it very clear that absolutely no one would be outside our perimeter at night. And now, at a meeting of all platoon leaders and NCO's, I very formally announced that no one would avail themselves of the services of the ladies. (You have to do things like that when you're the boss, and besides, it was army policy. LOL)

I also announced that SSG Allan and the motor sergeant would drive down to the hooch, a distance of perhaps 50 meters, each morning in C-10, the 1st platoon's jeep. Their orders were to make sure that no GI was in the joint. So, each morning about 10 a.m., our two heroes would drive down, each with a cup of coffee, rev up the engine (which had no muffler) to let the madam know they were there, then pass the time of day with her (while belt buckles were being fastened and boots were hitting the floor). Did I tell you there was a back door? And while the ladies were there, we never had a case of venereal disease since I'd arranged for the special forces medic to check the girls weekly and to keep their shots current.

It was all quite funny, the kids got laid, the girls made money, command did its job, all is well. Our illustrious first sergeant never did seem to understand the what and why of my actions in the matter. He just couldn't figure out my logic. And, LTC Rodolph couldn't figure out how we had no VD in this period because 2-3 cases per month were the norm for that size unit. I did tell him years later.

The fun ends here, unfortunately. After about 3 weeks, there was an explosion in the hootch about 2200. There had been some kind of meeting inside and someone had set off a hand grenade at waste level. There were a great many seriously wounded Vietnamese, all with gut wounds. The medic came running and I watched him perform some amazing emergency surgery. I think his name was Specialist Norman Billingsley. Those SF medics were better than many doctors in my book.

How good the medics all over Vietnam were was proven a couple of years later when I was stationed at Fort Hood. A terrible earthquake had occurred in Nicaragua and the staff at the Fort Hood base hospital was to be sent as part of the relief efforts. But some had to be left behind to handle emergencies. So who did they pick? All the medics who had been in 'Nam. That was a demonstration of trust and faith.

Incredible Bravery

There was a major enemy action to the North that night and helicopter gunships were returning to Phu Hiep Army Airfield to re-arm. There were no medevac birds normally available for Vietnamese civilians. Their priority order was U.S., allies and operatives, and then Vietnamese soldiers. No priority for Vietnam civilians. However, most of the pilots returning to base knew of the 577th since we'd built their airfield and facilities.

Fortunately, we were able to land enough Huey gunships and slicks under total blackout conditions to evacuate 23 seriously wounded people back to the 91st Evac Hospital at Phu Hiep. The ships had to come in without landing or running lights due to the very real danger of being fired on from the adjacent mountain jungle. As each aircraft indicated that they were on final approach, our coordinates and elevation would be repeated and the headlights my jeep would be quickly flashed once to guide them in. After all, they had a whole runway and adjacent area to choose from, so several aircraft could be on the ground at the same time.

The worst part was that, due to the way these ships were configured, we could only lie one gut-shot patient in each one, except for the few slicks, which could hold three.

There was one pilot who had requested the lights several times but was unable to see the site. I was getting nervous about all this exposure, expecting attack. Finally, I told him we'd try just one more time and if he failed to see us, he could abort and go on back to Phu Hiep. I was standing at the rear of my jeep when my driver flashed the lights again.

The nose of the helicopter was just a few feet in front of me, about 3 feet off the ground. In that instant of reflected light I saw a terrified face through the windshield. The lights went off and the bird hit the ground with a big thump. When I got over my own shock, I went to the pilot's window and asked if he was okay. He shook his head 'No' and I thought I could smell something. Turns out he'd not reset his altimeter when he had taken off and thought he was about 1,500 feet higher than he really was. I couldn't hear his engine or rotors due to the noise of the other aircraft on the ground. It was a wonder he hadn't hit a mountain or one of the other helicopters on the way in. It could have been a disaster but we lucked out. Anyway, he was able to safely take off with a casualty soon after.

I don't remember just how many Hueys landed in the dark that night. There was too much going on to count. But one thing I do know, and that is that each and every pilot who, by his own choice, decided to risk everything, including his crew, in order to try and save critically injured Vietnamese civilians. This shows just how brave these men were.

Other Happenings

I was visiting the special forces team one afternoon, sitting on the porch of the team house, which had been there since the French built it in the '50's. All the windows were covered with steel shutters to discourage snipers, but the porch was nice. As I sat there with a few of the team having a beer, I noticed an accurized M1 rifle leaning on the wall. I asked to

see it and looked out through the scope. As I put it down, one of the team sergeants took it and scanned the area. Surprisingly, he saw an NVA soldier coming out of the jungle about a thousand yards out. He chambered a round, took aim while sitting and popped him. Hell of a shot.

Nearby the team house was a tower of about 40 feet in height, also built by the French, that was used to spot approaching enemy, and also to get the azimuth to any target. It was equipped with lights so that Air Force fighter bombers could drop their ordnance more accurately at night.

The tower was also an occasional target itself when the enemy fired at it with a recoilless rifle from a nearby mountain. They never fired more than one shot at a time because the backblast from the weapon gave away the firing location. Unfortunately on one occasion our motor pool was in direct line of the incoming round, which missed the tower and hit

the motor sergeant's desk and coffee pot. He had just left to do something so he escaped injury, but he sure was mad about that coffee pot.

Puff The Magic Dragon

One night I heard what sounded like a freight train overhead. I came out of my tent and saw "Puff the Magic Dragon" doing his job about a mile away. I'd seen them before at Phu Hiep but only while they dropped illumination flares. Also known as a dragon ship with the call sign "Spooky," this was an AC-47 equipped with gatling guns firing from the door. A steady stream of tracers looked like a stream of fire from the air, all centered on the same area. Rumor had it that if Spooky fired at a football field, there wouldn't be a square inch that was not hit. I don't know if that is true, but I do know that the next day I saw a piece of belt buckle and was told it was all that was left of an NVA company. Awesome.

My Buddy

Even in war, nice things do happen. And here is one of them.

This is one of the local village children who wasn't afraid to come see the Americans. He liked to ride with me and got a big kick out of wearing my helmet.

Blonde Visitor

Towards the end of August, I had flown back to battalion headquarters for a meeting. Just before I was ready to return, Uncle Carl asked if there was anything we needed up at Dong Tre. I thought for a moment and then asked for a special visitor, if possible.

Just a few days later we got a radio message that said "Your tall blonde friend, your pad in zero-thirty mike."

Well, that took no decoding. It meant that a gorgeous blonde Australian stripper (who had performed at the base camp 3 times already and whom I'd never seen) was enroute and would land in 30 minutes.

I called in all the troops and had a flatbed trailer parked by the mess tent with half a dozen guys nailing down sheets of plywood for a stage. As the chopper landed and I escorted her into the perimeter, she asked for a place to change. She was wearing jungle fatigues and carrying a very small purse. I told her she could change in the mess tent and she handed me a reel-to-reel tape, saying, "I'm sure you can set this up for me."

In less than a minute, someone provided a tape deck and loaded it. And just as the steps to her stage were being completed, she stepped out in a full length gown that was very transparent. Pretty obvious why it fitted in that bag!

Once on stage, her music began and she started dancing. In less than 30 seconds she had dropped the gown and was entirely nude.

Did I mention that she was gorgeous, stacked like a brick shithouse and over 6 feet tall?

All the men were sitting on a hillside rising above the stage, and as she dropped the gown, there was a collective gasp from all. I was a bit worried that all these horny guys might get out of hand, but no, they were perfect gentlemen. Or perhaps they were spellbound.

In any case, she performed for nearly an hour to the delight of all. And towards the end, I ripped my eyes away and looked over at the perimeter wire. There were about 40 Montagnard men gawking and having the time of their life. At perhaps 5 feet tall and never having seen a round eye in their life, they probably thought they had died and gone to heaven. But their ecstasy was short-lived because very soon after, their wives appeared on the scene and the men were beaten soundly and forced back to their village.

I may not be accurate on the numbers, but I do know that she had a sliding scale for her fee, depending on the type of unit and location. Her fee might be $500 for 30 minutes for a garrison unit such as a supply company or other common unit. For an aviation unit, however, the sky was the limit. She figured they got paid extra and could afford it. But for special forces, she never charged a penny. Same for engineers in the field. And for the latter two, the show was almost an hour.

Thank you, June Collins. We loved you.

Resupply

Company C got its resupply via the choppers that brought folks from the battalion and higher commands. Team A-222 and their CIDG were

usually resupplied by an airdrop from a Caribou. This was always interesting because the plane made only one pass to do his LOLEX, or low level extraction. This was because of the risk of enemy fire if he made more than one pass. We normally were informed of an approaching plane about 5 minutes out.

Okay, that made sense, but it also made for some crazy drops. The idea is that a special parachute is used to open just before the palletized cargo hits the ground, slowing it down That means that the pilot has to be at the right elevation or problems occur. The Caribous dropped ammunition, clothing, weapons, rations and rice.

The picture above shows the plane pulling up, but he was too low for
the parachutes to open and the cargo splatted.

On one occasion, the pilot missed his drop zone and about a ton of
rice hit the ground and burst right behind my jeep, with the forward mo-
tion throwing most of it into the jeep. And whenever a load of rice burst,
the villagers would run out and collect as much as they could. I saw the
local Catholic priest take off his black pajama bottoms, tie the cuffs, and
fill them with rice. Funny as hell.

Sometimes this method of delivery really went wrong. I once
watched as a Caribou came in and dropped a load of 105 mm howitzer
ammo some 300 yards north of the DZ, near the jungle. The SF guys ran
for it, but the NVA came out of the jungle and got to the load first. After a
brief firefight they toted off their booty.

Dong Tre was an amazing experience for all who were there. The
area was surrounded by the elements of the 95th NVA Regiment and they
could have overrun both us and SF team A-222 anytime they wished —
and if they were willing to pay the price. It was interesting, though, that
there seemed to be an unspoken truce every Sunday. Company C took

the day off and there never was an enemy incident on that day of the week.

Company C company was probed a couple of times while we were there, but none of our guys were killed or wounded while I was there. A few mortar rounds had hit the special forces ammo storage area, but never Company C. The only unfortunate incident occurred one night when our perimeter was being probed and an assistant squad leader, a SGT E-5, was not with his squad on the perimeter. His platoon leader found him drunk and cowering under his bunk. The next day he was sent back to battalion along with a message that court martial orders would be forthcoming.

The day after that we got a message that MAJ Guba, the S-3, would visit to check on our progress with the airfield. Nothing unusual there, but when the Huey landed, he got out of one side and the sergeant got out of the other. I asked Guba what the hell was going on and he told me that the man was being returned to duty. We got into a real pissing contest with me ordering the man back in the chopper and telling my driver to shoot him if he got out, which I seriously meant. The good major went berserk over my countermanding his orders, but this was one of those times to "Bet yer bars."

In no uncertain terms, I told the major that though he outranked me, as S-3, he was NOT in my chain of command and had absolutely no authority in this case, since I was the man's commanding officer and I worked directly for the battalion commander and not him. Boy, was he mad, but he knew I was right and had to back down. I'm sure we would have crossed swords again, but he rotated home soon after.

Fougasse For The Artillery

Towards the latter part of August, A Battery of the 6/32nd Artillery Battalion moved into the Dong Tre firebase, replacing a ROK 155mm battery. The new battery had four 8-inch howitzers and a single 175mm gun.

The battery was used to moving and soon had their fortifications completed. The 8-inch howitzer was the most accurate artillery piece in Vietnam, but it did not have the range of the 175, which could shoot out to a range of 32,800 meters (20 miles), twice as far as the 8-inch How-itzers.

Once set up, the battery was firing missions nearly 24 hours per day. You got used to the rhythm of the firing and soon learned to speak only in the intervals between rounds.

Our company was above the level of the artillery and whenever the 175 would fire over us, you could actually see the round coming out of the barrel. And just as soon as the gun fired, the barrel would automatically drop to the horizontal position for reloading. They must have been firing very close to us because, on several occasions, I saw them fire, saw the round and then daylight through the barrel just as it began to drop. Awesome.

And then there was the day the 8-inchers were firing almost horizontally over their sandbag emplacements. I had just driven into the arty compound when a gun fired, ripping the top off one of the jeep radio antennas. Fortunately, these weapons all have a bore-riding safety pin which prevents the round arming itself until after leaving the barrel. That, plus the time it takes for the pin to fly out means the round is well clear of the barrel before it arms itself, and obviously the antenna was within that safe distance. It was pretty damn loud as well.

In the short time both units were at Dong Tre, I got to know the battery commander quite well. He was naturally concerned about security as artillery batteries were excellent NVA/VC targets. He wanted to know how to make fougasse, a flame mine. So I showed him.

First, we mixed the fougasse, which is gasoline and a thickener agent, which basically makes napalm. Then we took a used 8-inch brass shell casing, put a small C-4 charge in the bottom, put a used 155 casing inside that with a thermite grenade in it, and poured the napalm in. The C-4 had been rigged with a blasting cap inside and the firing wires fed outside the conglomeration. The whole thing was put in a shallow hole on the enemy side of a tree.

Now it gets interesting. The wires he was going to use to set it off were from a claymore mine and had been used several times, which meant the length was a lot less than they should have been. I told my friend I'd go get a new set of wires to splice in and make it all safe, but he said that it was long enough.

I didn't like this at all and told him not to set the damned thing off until I was up the hill a ways, and that I was going to take his picture to send his family.

This was the picture. You can't really see him, but the good captain is just this side of the blast in the left center of the picture. The tree saved his butt, but as he ran, chunks of napalm seemed to follow his ever step. I doubt he ever used a short detonator wire again.

Career Planning

I flew back to the base camp to discuss the next mission for Company C. LTC Rodolph called me up to his trailer (with air conditioning yet!) and we discussed the mission. It seemed as though we would be tasked to extend route 6B all the way to Pleiku, which would be very tough and dangerous. Instead, that mission was left for later and Company C was to relocate to Vung Ro Bay to replace Company B.

After settling the plans for our move, we had a chat about his and my careers. He told me he was going to come back to Vietnam and command an airborne engineer battalion. I replied that no one got two battalion commands. But he was confident, that was for sure. He considered Vietnam to be his war. When we were about finished talking, he said that the best thing I could do for my career was to hitch my star to a fast moving lieutenant colonel. I said, "Okay, Colonel. Hang tight."

In 1970, LTC Rodolph was stationed in DC. I looked him up and he invited me to dinner at his home. When I got there I found he had 4 boys, one of whom could not walk. He was about 5 or 6 years old and had to drag himself on the floor to get around. Carl's wife was lovely, but looked harried. We had a nice dinner and he told me he still planned on going back as a battalion commander yet again. I still didn't believe he could do that and I was concerned that he seemed not to consider his family.

Around Christmas of 1971 I was on an ROTC assignment at the University of Missouri-Rolla. A phone call from Rodolph really surprised me. He told me that he was returning to Vietnam as the C.O. of the 326th Combat Engineer Battalion (Airborne) in the 101st Airborne Division. That was hard enough for me to believe, but he said he wanted me to come with him and be his S-3. This whole thing amazed me, and was hard to grasp. I told him that I had gotten half way through a masters degree in computer science on a part time basis and the Army had agreed to give me the remaining time and pay for the rest of the degree. He said he'd make sure I came right back after the tour. I reminded him that I was still a captain (the promotion list to major was frozen) and that an S-3 was a major's job. He said not to worry, he would make sure of the assignment. I said needed time to think and asked him to call me back the next day.

After talking it over with my wife, I decided not to accept. It really was a great honor, but I wanted that degree and really didn't want to go back to Nam, though I knew at some point I would have to. When he called, I told him no and why, but thanked him very much. He never spoke to me again.

And yes, he did go do just what he said. The only time I saw him again was on television when he was filmed greeting Bob Hope who had come to the 101st Airborne for his annual Christmas show.

Carl Rodolph has passed now, so R.I.P. Boss. We'll have a drink someday down the road to toast that second command.

A Fast Exit

We finished the airfield on 28 August. Everything was kept totally secret about the move for absolute security.

The platoon leaders and NCOs were briefed about 0230 on the morning of 29 August and the troops awakened at 0300. Everything was loaded up and we left at 0500. The last thing done was to set off all the claymore mines that had been set in concrete. And we did leave the pre-fabricated CP for whomever wanted it.

We headed down 2-D to those fireworks and the convoy was soon spread out over 10 kilometers for security. By being fast and secret I hoped we would be gone before the enemy could get his act together to ambush us on the road.

We were unable to arrange for air cover but still needed a FAC, or forward air controller. LTC Rodolph volunteered himself for the job. He was in the co-pilot's seat of a Mohawk from the 225th, with the antenna of an AN-PRC 25 stuck out the window. The OV-1 is a pretty fast airplane, so with the limited range of the prick 25 I had little time to talk to him because the OV-1 covered that 10 km in no time at all. It was a bizarre situation, but things worked and the Boss had a ball playing FAC.

This is the completed runway shown above the special forces camp.

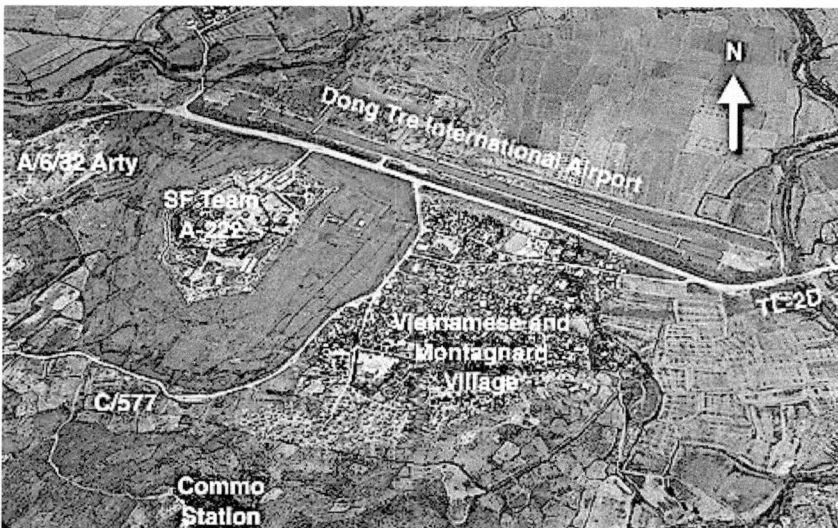

Company C positions are on the hill in the lower left of the picture. The trail goes up the 142 meter high hill to the communications outpost. The far left area was the artillery firebase.

The village in the center is an unusual mixture of both Vietnamese and Montagnards. The two usually disliked one another, but it worked out here. The picture was taken just before Company C departed. I am told that this camp later became the headquarters of the 95th NVA Regiment.

Chapter 4 - Vung Ro Bay (Sep - Nov)

Company C moved to Port Lane at Vung Ro Bay without incident on 29 August. We settled in the two story barracks and admin buildings left by Company B, who's major mission at the port was building the De-Long Pier Causeway and the access road to the South beach where the port transportation company was located.

The causeway would later be washed out during typhoon Freida which occurred in November, but was replaced soon thereafter.

Our new mission was completing construction of the 380 man cantonment at Port Lane and maintaining QL-1. The earthmoving platoon was attached to the 572d Engr Co. and utilized in the development of the Chop Chai Quarry. This new set of jobs looked to be far less exciting than being at Dong Tre. There were going to be moments of interest, to say the least.

Here is what part of the Chop Chai quarry looked like after it got going.

The quarry was primarily used in support of the resurfacing of QL-1. It began with a 75 ton per hour crusher and eventually got up to 225 tons per hour.

There was an old French train there that ran on narrow gauge tracks. It was used to carry crushed rock out to the highway and elsewhere because the huge dump trucks used there were too heavy to drive on the road, even when empty. On two occasions I saw one of the dump trucks back up to an old ore car and dump its load a bit too fast. That had the effect of turning that "toy train" over on its side. To fix the problem, the truck would drive around the other side of the train and carefully push the cars back upright. The rock would be reloaded by front end loaders. Quite the site.

There was also an Army Security Agency radio station on top of the 391 meter high mountain, and the Viet Cong were often in between the top and bottom.

This is a current picture. The radio tower was not there in '67.

Enemy Attacks

Intelligence sources had indicated that a division of NVA and VC units were located in the hill mass surrounding the Tuy Hoa Valley to the North, West and South. The mission of these enemy units was to disrupt the national elections, tax the local populace, capture the rice harvest, disrupt lines of communications, and harass the Free World Forces within the province. The elections were to be held on 1 September.

The 577th and attached units were actively engaged in direct contact with the enemy or on a full alert status on 13 of the 15 nights during the period 30 August through 13 September. The battalion experienced light attacks on the Phu Hiep quarry, the Highway QL-1 borrow pit, convoys on Highway QL-1, the base camp and perimeter, as well as heavy attacks on the 553rd Engineer Company (Float Bridge) security force on the Song Ban Thach bridge site. The bridge itself was comprised of M4T6 float bridging over the water and Bailey Bridge over the island section about ⅔ of the way across from the North.

The 553rd had been assigned the mission of securing the site since the installation of the bridge the previous year. At this time the commander was CPT Keith Larson. At 2330 on 30 August the bridge came under sniper fire. Then, at 0100 the next morning, the bridge was attacked by an estimated VC/NVA company from the South shore using mortars, automatic weapons, concussion charges and satchel charges. The enemy overran south shore defensive positions and repelled a charge from the North shore. A quick reaction force from the company successfully repulsed the attack. Gunships supported the action.

Master Sergeant Julian Hooper, Sergeant Farrell Richard Carew and Private First Class Edward Lee Rankin, all of the 553rd, were killed in action. There others were wounded. Enemy casualties were unknown.

After the first attack LTC Rodolph had D7 dozers clear the fields of fire around the bridge, including removing some mud-walled thatched roof houses adjacent to the bridge.

The next evening beginning at 2205, several attempts were made to infiltrate both north and south shore positions. An attack on the South shore began at 2218 but was repulsed by M-79 grenade fire. At approximately midnight some 30 Viet Cong were observed through a starlight infrared scope assembling on the Southwest shore and were fired upon. Four enemy were seen swimming in the river and attempting to blow the floating bridge, but were driven off with automatic weapons fire and grenades. Eight Viet Cong were KIA (body count), 1 WIA (actual) and 20 more estimated to be wounded.

LT David A. Pugh displayed real courage when he engaged a large number of the enemy using a starlight scope with excellent results. I am sure he saved many American lives that night.

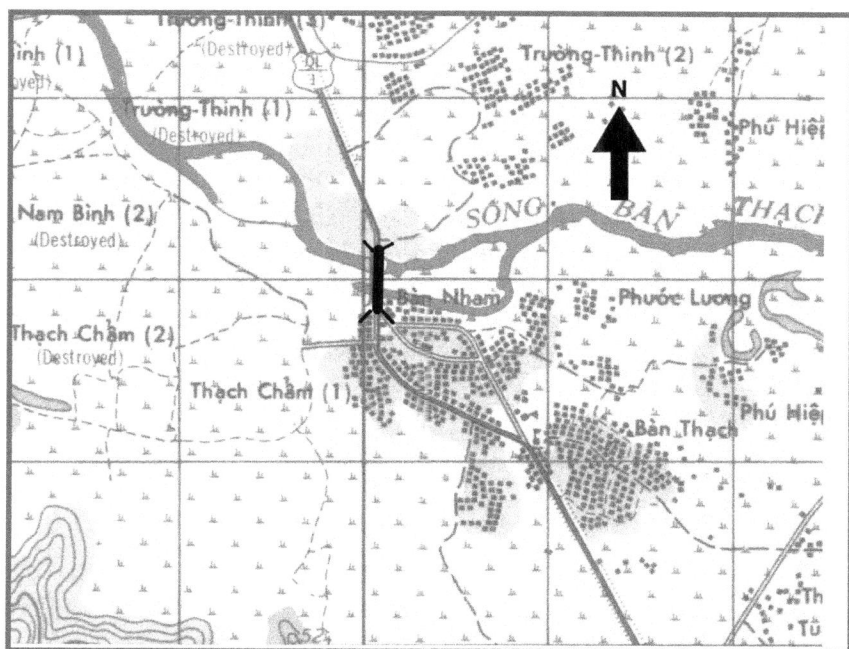

Company C was placed in a general reserve status on 1 September.

At 0230 on 2 September, enemy automatic weapons fire was directed against the North shore positions from about 75 meters to the East. An attack was attempted but was driven off. Harassing fire continued through the night. One enemy was KIA and 1 WIA.

On 6 September at about 2350, the site was attacked by an estimated VC/NVA company from the vicinity of the market place in the Ban Nham village on the South shore using B40 rockets, automatic weapons and M-79 fire. This was repulsed by quad.50 cal, 40 mm Duster, heavy automatic weapons and M-79 fire. At 2400 gunships were called in to fire on suspected enemy positions. Three friendly were wounded and the enemy had 1 KIA and 1 WIA.

Companies B and D took over nighttime security responsibilities from the 553rd for two weeks beginning on 9 September.

On 11 September LTC John R. McDonald succeeded LTC Rodolph as the battalion commander.

On 18 September at about 0600 hours and estimated NVA company approached the bridge from the North ran into U.S. and PF (popular force militia) defensive positions and was repulsed. The action continued in the form of a 3-day stalemate until the 20th Regimental Combat Team (RCT) Republic of Korea Army (ROK) conducted a series of operations known as TAKABI III, sweeping up from the South to clear the village.

During this time Company B was deployed as infantry in a blocking position to prevent the enemy from advancing toward the bridge. Company C was alerted to reinforce the ROK from the South if needed. No casualties were reported.

Sporadic harassing fire was received from 20 September until 15 October when the security responsibility was passed to the 103 RF Company.

According to some who were in the firefights, the VC/NVA KIA was much higher but USARV insisted on actual body counts to give "credit." No one was interested in searching an active battle area and risking American lives just to count corpses. Who cared at that point?

Wild Ride

While on alert at Vung Ro Bay at the beginning of the ROK advance, I was ordered to come up to battalion headquarters, though I can't remember why. Seemed odd, but it must have been important given the situation at the time. I requested a helicopter but that was denied. So, into the jeep and off we go on the 20 km ride, including crossing the Song Ban Thach Bridge. This must have been on 18 September because things at the bridge had been quiet for several days. I sure wouldn't have gone had I known what I was getting into.

The Koreans had established a roadblock at their compound south of the river just down the mountain. When we arrived there 3 Korean APCs were lined up to go north. I asked permission of an english speaking ROK colonel to join them. He pretended not to understand and indicated we should go back south. I tried several times to communicate, but gave up. We sat in the jeep while I thought about the situation.

The roadblock was suddenly removed and the three tracks started up QL-1. Seemed like good security to me, so we sped past the guards and pulled in behind the last APC as I climbed into the back of the jeep and manned the M-60 machine gun. No problem. At least until we came close to the Ban Nham village and all 3 tracks suddenly drove off the road and advanced on line through the rice paddies. Whoops. Not good.

But there was no fire from the village at first, so it seemed better to continue on than to sit between two ROK units. I told my driver to go as fast as he could, but his foot was already on he floor. Then, just as we entered the village we started taking fire at about the same time the.50 cals on the APCs opened up. I spun the gun to reply to our shooter as we roared around a bend, throwing me off balance. This happened several times and I was mostly just hanging onto the gun instead of really returning fire.

Just as the firefight started, I heard a frantic voice on the radio requesting an airborne troop drop because NVA tanks were approaching from the South! Huh? Some idiot thought my jeep was a tank?

A few moments later we roared up to the South end of the bridge where good old COL Bullmoose, I mean Hospelhorn, was sitting was on top of a quad.50 gun truck with all barrels aimed right at us! Shit.

We skidded to a sidewise halt just in front of the truck's bumper. I looked up at the colonel, saluted somewhat sarcastically, and told him that the road was clear of tanks. It's a wonder the S.O.B. didn't blow us to hell just for spite. Probably would have given himself a medal.

Never did get to battalion that day.

New Commander

LTC MacDonald was told about the monsoon rains and how difficult it was to work on QL-1 during that time. Well, he promptly denied that it rained so much, saying that he, as a soils engineer knew it couldn't be correct. Or something like that. He said we were spending too much effort on road maintenance.

Hmmm, he was the commander so we cut back on the work, but he sure was dead wrong. The monsoon would resume in October and continue until February or March. There would be about 4 days of pleasant weather just before the monsoon, and 4 days at the end. Hot as hell or drenched in near constant heavy rain, that was the weather in Phu Yen province.

MacDonald would learn, but he was always a grouch who knew it all. A very difficult man to work for.

Bailey Bridge

I woke up to a huge explosion very early one morning. As soon as I heard it, I knew that the double-single Bailey Bridge just down the mountain over the Song Cua River towards the ROK camp on QL-1 had been blown up. Again.

At first light the area was secured and, once again, the guys had to do a mine sweep. This was really weird because the blown bridge was over a shallow river and there was a dry bypass dirt road previously created by Company B, it not just yet being the monsoon season. It was pretty obvious that Charlie had done this for a second time to embarrass the Korean troops who were supposed to secure this area and the bridge. They would pay dearly for their lack of action.

As I began to study the damage, it was obvious that the underside of the bridge needed to be examined. That quickly showed that there was at least one more demolition charge there. I sure wished we had someone else trained in demolitions, but the Army never thought construction troops needed that little skill. That left me. So, I clambered up into the

substructure towards the first charge I could see. Nervous? Me nervous? Sweating bullets is more like it. I was really, really hoping that the charge didn't have an electric detonator that was still hot. I had visions of Chuck sitting up the mountain just waiting to finish the job.

When I got to the first charge, I could see that it was connected by detonating cord to another one on the adjacent corner. Great. After cutting the Det cord on both sides of the first charge, it was off to the next one. Same story. A third charge was on the last corner. Shit!

Finally, all three charges were safely off the bridge and I could see where the one that had gone off was detonated by a fuse, not an electric setup. The det cord from charge 1 to 2 failed for some reason and that kept 2, 3, and 4 from exploding

Each charge weighed 20 kilograms (42 pounds) and had all 4 gone off, the bridge would have really been a mess. Yeh, but much easier to replace than fix like it was.

I love the thought of several little NVA soldiers toting that Chinese dynamite all the way down the Ho Chi Minh Trail, and having some Sergeant say, "It didn't work, Nguyen, you and the boys go back and get some more."

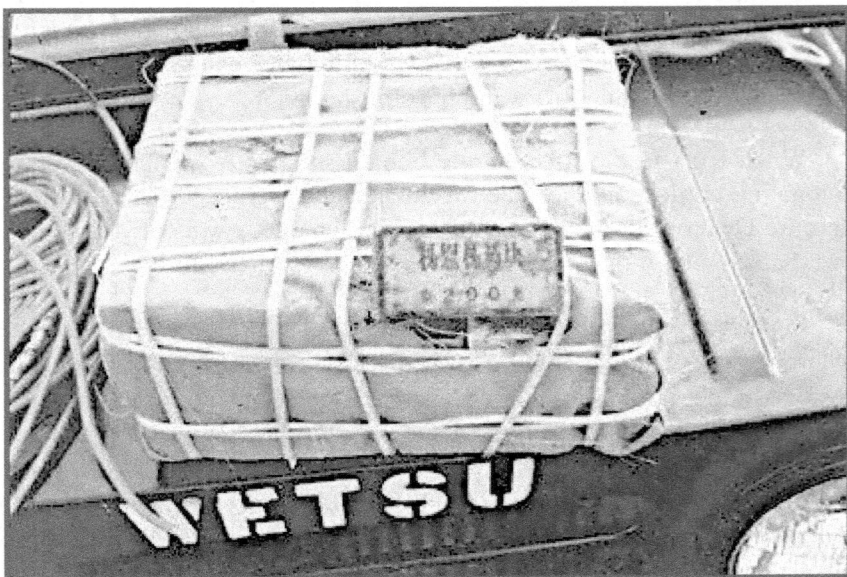

You're wondering what WETSU means? "We eat this shit up!"

Traffic on QL-1 wasn't delayed at all, since they had the bypass to get around our repair work. That consisted of bringing a 20-ton truck-mounted crane in to lift the busted end of the bridge while we replaced the damaged panels. The crane was working at its absolute limit, so the lift was very slow and careful.

All of a sudden, there was a tremendous bang. No one knew what had happened.

Then we realized that the ground had sheared beneath the left side front outrigger. These are big hydraulically controlled pads that stabilize the crane. The outrigger had dropped almost 4 inches. But what had made so much noise?

Soon enough, we found that the A-frame inside the crane had bent. That thing was what made the crane capable of lifting. The operator very slowly exited the cab because the whole crane just might have collapsed.

Another crane was brought in to take some of the damaged crane's load so that the bridge could be carefully lowered back down. After removing the first crane, the load bearing area was reinforced with steel plates over wood beams. Cautiously, the crew made the lift again.

Miraculously, the maintenance guys found a new A-frame in only 2 days.

Bullmoose showed up again that evening with a few of his infantry troops. He said he'd been in the engineers in World War II and was "going to remind Charlie that we were still around."

The next thing I knew, he had the 50's shooting up the mountainside behind us. He was known for playing soldier like this, but this time his guns hit the top of the crane. Another delay. This guy was a complete idiot.

The next morning, soon after work resumed, the Commanding General of the Korean White Horse Division showed up and brought the Captain who was C.O. of the ROK company mentioned earlier. Work slowed and then stopped as we watched this Major General berate his subordinate.

Suddenly the general drew his.45 Colt pistol and began to beat the poor captain with the butt of the weapon. I desperately wanted to do something, but I knew I couldn't stop what was going on. It would have caused an international incident and my own court-martial. The captain was nearly dead when the beating stopped.

I found out later that, as punishment, the entire infantry company was sent back to South Korea in shame. Talk about losing face!

Another one of my reasons for not jumping in to stop the beating was that I had previously driven by the ROK camp and seen the company formed up to witness some miscreant beaten with a board for God knows what minor offense. I'll never understand the oriental mindset.

Despite the delays, we had the bridge repaired and operational in about 3 days. WETSU!

The 173rd Arrives - Don't tell

On 15 September 1967, the headquarters and other elements of the 173rd Airborne Brigade had moved into the base camp. The 577th Engineer Battalion was placed in general support of the 173rd for Operation Bolling.

But before that happened, CPT Ken Jobe, the battalion Assistant S-3 and acting S-2 (Intelligence) was on the airfield when a C-130 landed. And out of the back of it comes a captain with a jeep, and an NCO, and a trailer. And all the markings are obliterated.

CPT, "We're here."

Jobe, "Well, that's nice."

CPT, "No wait, we're here."

Jobe, "Wonderful, I'm here too. I don't know why you are here."

CPT, "You didn't know we were coming?"

Jobe, "No. Don't have the foggiest idea. Who are you?"

CPT, "Well, I can't tell you. You're supposed to meet us here."

Jobe, "No, man, we're building this airfield. I don't really know about what you're doing. I mean, you want to get on the airplane and fly back out that's fine with me, but who are you trying to find?"

CPT, "Well, aren't you with the area command? Don't you know we're coming? And aren't you supposed to meet us?"

Jobe, "Look, why don't you get off the airfield so we can continue construction. I really would appreciate it if you'd move that piece of trash out of here."

It turns out it was the lead element of the 173rd Airborne Infantry Brigade. Part of the brigade was going to Highway 7B, and they're going to conduct a sweep up there, like they'd done a couple years before, looking for the bad guys.

And that was how Ken became the Eighteenth Engineer Brigade liaison officer to the 173rd. And you also can see some of the thought process of the 173rd idea of cooperation.

When the rest of the brigade came to town on the 17th, it was pretty funny. Unit sleeve patches were taped over and vehicle numbers were covered with tied on sandbags. There were just a few clues about the unit ID, however. They landed in C-130's with just a few vehicles. Every soldier wore jump wings. And an "X" could be seen on some bumpers, meaning an independent brigade. Duh, it just *might* be the 173rd , since they were the only separate airborne brigade in-country. A final clue was that you could see the outline of the unique 173rd patch under the tape.

Who were they fooling? The Viet Cong and NVA certainly knew who they were. They knew damned near every thing before it happened!

Some of the troopers seemed to think that Phu Hiep was an R&R location, especially since there was a beach. Unfortunately, the surf could be rough and the brigade was warned about sharks. They ignored the advice, as they often did, and there were shark bites.

Anyway, their troops had no club facilities, so the 577th nicely invited them to share ours. Sadly, quite a few Sky Soldiers decided that they didn't want to walk back to their area, so they would steal some jeeps and drive back. The jeeps were not returned, of course, and their officers seemed to think it was quite funny. Asking for their help in stopping it didn't do anything.

After a couple of weeks of this, the brigade provost marshal stormed into the battalion headquarters, demanding to know where his jeep was. What jeep? No one knew anything about it, of course. It was several days before the jeep was found on top of a short water tower. And, due to the battalion's extremely heavy military construction responsibilities at the time, it was several days more before a crane could be spared to lower the vehicle back to terra firma. How it had gotten up on that tower was never explained, but no more vehicles were stolen from our camp. Ahh, the sweet taste of revenge.

Construction of ten helipads, an ammunition supply point, a tactical operations center, and latrine, and shower facilities were accomplished in performing the general support mission. Two major tactical support mission would be accomplished by the battalion in the initial phases of Operation Bolling.

Operation Bolling

This operation ran from 19 Sep 1967 until 31 Jan 1968. The 173rd was assigned the mission of protecting the rice harvest in Phu Yen province. One battalion of the brigade had this mission. The rest of the brigade moved to Kontum as a FSB for the upcoming debacle at Dak To.

The intelligence (?) officer and other 173rd staff asked where the Viet Cong were. They asked special forces, U.S. ARVN advisors, they even asked the 577th. The answer? "Out in the valley collecting rice." The brains in the brigade said their intelligence indicated the enemy was in the mountains around the valley.

Oh, did you happen to notice the mission of the battalion a couple of paragraphs above? Didn't bother the brains in the least.

From the book, Dak To, by Edward F. Murphy: "Combat in the Tuy Hoa area usually consisted of brief contact with small bands of VC. The squads of a rifle platoon would set up ambushes along likely avenues of VC movement. Then they'd wait for someone to walk into the trap.

The 173d's rifle companies spent a great deal of time patrolling in the coastal mountain ranges of Phu Yen. Though not nearly as rugged as Dak To's mountains, these ranges provided the enemy with plenty of opportunities for concealment. The Sky Soldiers had to go in and root out the VC. Sometimes they were successful, sometimes they weren't."

Gee, why weren't the Sky Soldiers out in the valley? Oh, yeah, their intelligence, or lack thereof.

On 18 September a task force whose lead element from Company D conducted a road clearing and repair mission on Route 7B to Cung Son special forces camp, some 50 kilometers away. The mission to enable Battery C, 6/32 Artillery, to move its 8 inch and 175 mm howitzers into position. Then they were to escort Company D of the 14th Engineer Battalion, which had been cut off at Cung Son, back to Tuy Hoa. The 173rd was to provide security.

CPT Jobe, in his role the 18th Engineer Brigade liaison officer to the 173rd Airborne Brigade, had argued long and hard with Brigadier General Schweiter and his S-3 about how to get in and out of Cung Son quickly and safely, to no avail. The brigade leaders were insistent that this dangerous road march be conducted at the infantry walking speed of 4 mph, while CPT Jobe made the proven case for the engineer speed of 20 mph and unannounced. He was unsuccessful. It seems that in this case and later at the terrible battle of Dak To, the airborne way was always right even when disastrously wrong. General Schweiter, to his credit, had won a Silver Star in WWII and another in Korea, but now he was an opinionated and extremely stubborn man. So was his operations officer.

The 173rd was in charge and all the bad guys knew what was going on. CPT Doug Booth, *(KIA 12 May 1970 on his 2nd tour)*, C.O. of Company D had a group of engineers up front on the road doing clearance, but were slowed by the speed of the infantry behind them. Doug radioed back to the 173rd Cav squadron commander, and said, "Hey man, there's some guys in black pajamas up here in a bunch of spider holes. And, you know, we're clearing the road so the 173rd can come behind. But do you want us to engage them? What do you want us to do?" The Cav squadron commander said something like, "We want you to get out of the way. You ash and trash guys get the hell out of the way. We'll bring the Cav up there. We'll take care of them."

The major was killed a few minutes later. The jeep he was in was blown up and burned by an RPG. The 173rd lost three people that day The whole thing came to a screeching halt. What should have been a half-day trip in turned into a three or four-day exercise. And, it was not pleasant.

The 173rd escorted elements of the 553rd which was to build a bridge over a tributary to the Song Ban Thach River that Schweiter did not want to ford, insisting that an AVLB (Armored Vehicle Launched Bridge) be used. CPT Jobe had told him that those bridges were only found in armored engineer battalions and we couldn't get one, nor was it needed. The brigade staff then decided that we could build a float bridge across the stream.

The truck carrying a brand new load of M4T6 balk, to be used in building the bridge by hand, got a flat tire enroute. The airborne troopers simply dumped it into the adjacent canal and moved on. That was fine with the 553rd who didn't want to waste the time to build the bridge in the first place.

A short time later CPT Jobe was called to the heavily guarded McDonald's Office where there was LTC Lammie of the 14th, McDonald, our battalion XO MAJ Tener, the group C.O., and Larson's S-3. Jobe was told that Company D of the 14th, was "coming out of Cung Son," given the date, told to coordinate and plan with the 173rd, and that Jobe would be personally bringing Company D of the 14th out since the C.O of D/14th was to DEROS within 2 days and they had no replacement, only a very green second lieutenant and an outstanding First Sergeant. CPT Jobe was told not to assume command. "The Lieutenant and First Sergeant will be told to do what you say."

The next day Jobe used the 35th Group Huey to run a recon of 7B. The pilots would not get below 2500 feet. He wanted to be at 25 feet instead. They were afraid of being hit by.50 cal MG fire. The recon was a waste of time. It should be pointed out that both pilots of the group chopper were on their third tour, having flown both guns and slicks previously, and both had already been shot down 3 times each. Understandable caution, but not good for the recon.

Two days later Jobe rode the group's fixed wing Beaver into Cung Son and prepared to bring D/14th out. They were escorted by elements of the 173rd and an artillery battery. They forded the tributary to the Song Ban Thatch, taking two days to come out. Why so long? The 173rd was checking out each bush and moving really slow as a result of the Doug Booth experience. They did not move out of the artillery fan. Overnight, they laagered in a 360 degree defense in a cow pasture within the artillery fan. Next day when they were on the way out, CPT Booth's jeep, driven by Gary Vizioli, ran over a mine and was wrecked, though no one was hurt.

That's Gary on the chain hoist loading the jeep onto a truck. Doug Booth is third from the right.

I should point out that this jeep was brand new. I had worn out my old jeep and just before going to Company C, got a new one. Then they go and blow it up. Not very nice.

When the convoy got to the ambush site, the remains of the cav squadron jeep were observed, then they met a welcoming party from Tuy Hoa, consisting of government officials, young ladies with flowers. Seems rather strange that anyone cared, but perhaps it was just time for a politician to do something.

Operation Bolling went on until the beginning of Tet on 31 January 1968. Elements of the Brigade killed 705 enemy, apprehended 2488 suspects and captured 237 individual weapons. A number of civilians were killed, but these usually became Viet Cong in the official count. Friendly fire accounted for a number of dead and wounded paratroopers.

One major battle occurred during the Operation in January 1968 when the 4th Battalion, 503d Infantry decimated a Battalion from the 95th NVA Regiment at Tuy Hoa North Airfield, killing 189. This was one of the few times enemy troops in Phu Yen engaged in a set piece battle.

Dak To

The rest of the brigade flew to Kontum and began operations around Dak To. In some of the heaviest fighting seen in the Central Highlands area, heavy casualties were sustained by both sides in bloody battles around Dak To, about 280 miles north of Saigon near the Laotian border.

The 1,000 U.S. troops there were reinforced with 3,500 additional troops from the U.S. 4th Division and the 173rd Airborne Brigade. They faced four communist regiments of about 6,000 troops. The climax of the operation came in a savage battle from November 19-22 for Hill 875, 12 miles southwest of Dak To. The 173rd was victorious, forcing the North Vietnamese to abandon their last defensive line on the ridge of Hill 875, but the victory was a costly one because the paratroopers suffered the loss of 135 men, 30 of whom died as a result of an accidental U.S. air strike on U.S. positions. In the 19 days of action, North Vietnam fatalities were estimated at 1,455. Total U.S. casualties included 285 killed, 985 wounded, and 18 missing.

And then the 4,500 Allied troops pulled out. A hill was taken and then returned. This was done frequently, at great cost and with little to show for it.

It should be noted that nothing like 1,455 NVA bodies were seen. After every engagement only a few enemy bodies were found. And, according to the Army Reporter edition of 671231, "During 1967, paratroopers of the 173rd killed 1,778 enemy soldiers."

So, 1778 in total - 1455 at Dak To - 750 in Bolling = -427 net killed. Body counts are interesting, eh? No wonder we lost the war. We increased the number of enemy soldiers by killing them.

The Itschner Plaque

CPT Thomas E. Weber was the C.O. of the 173rd Airborne Engineer Company and acted as the Brigade Engineer for a while. He became a friend of mine before going to Dak To. His company was committed as infantry which is a last ditch effort when the infantry is being overrun. They suffered 6 KIA and 9 WIA. Tom was wounded and suffered a concussion. He later showed Ken Jobe the helmet he was wearing with a defanged CHICOM grenade, complete with wooden handle attached. The grenade was thrown at Tom, hit his helmet and lodged there, but did not explode.

During the battle of Dak To, the airborne engineers were recommended for one Distinguished Service Cross and earned one Silver Star, twelve Bronze Stars with "V" device, two Air Medals, and three Army Commendation Medals with "V" device. In support of other combat operations the engineers participated in during the year, they received 27 additional awards for valor.

His company was the 1967 recipient of the Itschner Plaque presented to the most outstanding U.S. Army engineer company of that year.

My P.O.W.

Back to Vung Ro: Coming south on QL-1 returning from battalion headquarters, where there was always some meeting the I had to go to, we drove by the ROK garbage dump adjacent to the road. There was a young boy of perhaps 14 poking around and putting something in his pocket. He seemed nervous, so we stopped and brought him to the jeep where he was searched. In his pockets were about half a dozen dead D-Cell flashlight batteries but no weapons.

It takes about 2-3 volts to set off a blasting cap. That's normally two good flashlight batteries, but if you solder half a dozen "dead" ones together, you'll make things go boom quite well.

The young man had enough English to try and tell me the batteries were for his flashlight. Not buying that one, so I put him in the back of the jeep and kept my M-16 on him as we returned to base camp.

The White Mice soon came and took the boy in tow, undoubtedly for some form of torture and perhaps death. I hated to give him to them, but we had no way to take care of prisoners, much less interrogate them. Sure as hell didn't trust the battalion interpreter.

One Dumb Soldier

A few weeks later, I was again wakened, this time by a shot. It turns out that one our young men had gotten up, got dressed, turned on the lights and said something to the effect of, "I'm getting out of this chicken shit outfit!" He then picked up his M16 and went out the door and down the steps. Another man ran after him and when he got to the top of the steps, saw the butt of an M16 showing around the corner of the building. It went off.

When I got there, the man was on the ground with a minor flesh wound through the fatty part of his side. I called for a Dustoff chopper and had him taken to the helipad. Just before the bird landed, I asked him why on earth he did this? He replied that it seemed a good way to go home. I told him it seemed a good way to go to jail.

And now the story gets really weird. He was taken to the 91st Evac to be patched up and I sent his court-martial charges up the next day. As it turns out, the Miranda decision had just been made by the Supreme Court and the U.S. Army had absolutely no idea what to do about it. Because of this, command refused to sign off on the charges. So, I demanded he be transferred, and he was, to Headquarters Company.

About a six weeks later, after turning over command of Company C to CPT Joe Larremore, I was reassigned as Assistant Operations Officer in Headquarters Company. You can see what's coming, right?

I was the battalion duty officer one night a few weeks later, which meant, amongst other things, I had to check the guards. So, I put down my coffee cup, picked up my weapon and walked out the door to a guard post a few yards from the headquarters building. And, inside a small rain shelter, sound asleep was... Yep, you got it. Dumdum himself. Snoring away.

This time, I decided to be a little more formal with the situation. I woke up the battalion's top NCO, the Sergeant Major, and had him return with me to our young friend, who was still stacking Z's.

The Sergeant Major was satisfied that this just might be an issue. So, with his agreement, I reached in and removed the M16 from our fearless guard's grip. He still didn't wake up!

Being a bit pissed, I pointed the rifle into the air and ripped off a few rounds. Slowly, he woke up and the last I saw of him, he was being dragged off by a rather large, very angry Sergeant Major.

Charges were again written up, but for some reason, things got delayed until it was time for me to go home. I was asked to stay for the court martial (no time frame), but I politely declined, leaving an affidavit instead.

You think this is over? Not yet. A month or so, later I was in the Career Course at Fort Belvoir, VA. And, returning from lunch with several friends, we listened to Paul Harvey on the car radio. As usual, he had an interesting story to end his show. This one was about a young soldier who had been court-martialed in Vietnam and given a dishonorable discharge.

Just before leaving the Army, he left the base, broke into a hardware store, setting off the alarms, of course. When the police arrived, he was found, stuck in the rafters. But, in his intelligent way, he managed to fall - to his death.

At this point I said, "I know who this is!", and at then Mr. Harvey gave his name. Hey, you figured it out again! Aren't you smart?

Amphibious Assault

Right after the attacks on the bridge had ended, the C.O. of the transportation company running Port Lane became concerned that the port might come under rocket fire from caves near the top of the mountain opposite the port. The Viet Cong were known to have used them before. In addition, a shipload of bombs for Tuy Hoa AFB was due to arrive soon.

Surely a job for the infantry, right? Well, the White Horse ROK had been up that way not too long before and were not interested. So who else would you ask? The Engineers, of course.

Okay, I say, "But how do we get over there? We are sure not gonna hump through the jungle for 10 miles to get there!" After some discussion, we decided the only practical way was to make use of a LARC (Lighter Amphibious Resupply Cargo), an amphibious vehicle used to lighter cargo from ships. Not an assault boat for sure. But, after we mounted a .50 cal MG on the bow for backup firepower, it was about the best we could do.

A call for volunteers provided about 20 men who were armed with M-16s and extra ammunition magazines. About 40 lbs of C-4 and necessary detonators were also brought. After a visual study with binoculars and locating the caves on a map, we boarded the LARC and crossed the bay. We made our "assault landing" by climbing down the sides of the LARC. The LARC was to station about 200 meters out in the bay and stay in radio contact in case we needed the .50 cal. I really hoped that wouldn't be necessary since visibility in the jungle would be poor. Man, was that an understatement!

The caves we were investigating were just below the second mountain top to the right in the previous picture. The jungle, though only a double-canopy, was thick and dark. The terrain was rough and steep so movement was slow. Using a compass to guide the team, we clambered our way up.

Near the top of the climb, I knew we were close to the objective but could not see the caves. I was concerned about our exact location in case we needed the heavy MG or artillery. So I asked for a volunteer to climb to the top of a tree that was about 80 feet tall and pop a smoke grenade so the LARC could confirm our location.

After about a 30 minute climb, our fearless young engineer troop was as high as he could go, about 70 feet. He popped the smoke and I notified the LARC to watch for it and confirm the color. The reason for the confirmation was that Charlie often listened to U.S. FM radio frequencies and would also ignite a smoke grenade to confuse the issue or set up an ambush. By getting confirmation of the smoke color things usually worked out better

The tree foliage was so thick and the humidity so high that it took more than 20 minutes for the smoke to climb above the trees. Our climber easily came back down first, but finally the RTO on the LARC confirmed yellow smoke and worked out our position. Amazingly, we were only about 20 meters from the caves! Charlie surely would have spotted us.

But, fortunately, we found no evidence of rockets in the caves, though it was quite apparent that the place had recently been used. So, after clambering back to the shore, we returned to the compound. I'm sure some of the young guys were disappointed that we found nothing, but I was quite pleased with that outcome.

Beach Time

In early October, a half day beach trip was arranged. Perhaps a dozen officers drove south of Vung Ro to where QL-1 starts to climb the mountain. This was the area where trucks returning from Nha Trang or Cam Rahn Bay always seemed to break down. And the entire area was owned by the Viet Cong, but they were active mostly at night.

But, just off the highway was one of the most beautiful little beaches I had ever seen. I am sure someone has built a hotel there by now.

The mob piled out and set up a grill for burgers and dogs, with a few cans of Pabst Blue Ribbon for hydration while we took turns manning that M-60 on my jeep for security. After lunch and a swim, Chaplain Jones asked me if I had a grenade in my jeep. Of course. Would I teach him how to throw one? Sure.

When I walked back down the beach with a couple of frags for Chaps, I noticed everyone else backing way up. Cowards, one and all. Chaps and I were now standing in the water a few inches above our ankles.

I explained how to hold the grenade, pull the pin and throw it, noting the 3-4 second safety time before detonation. Demonstration time, so I showed him how to hold the grenade and the handle, pulled the pin with my left hand, and then held the grenade. Again saying that as long as I held that handle against the grenade, nothing happens. I showed him how to put the pin back in.

Then I did it all again, this time throwing the grenade into the ocean about 30 feet away. Boom!

Trainee action time. Here's your grenade, Chaps. Go for it!

He couldn't pull the pin. The others are hiding behind the jeeps. I showed him how again, put the pin back in so it would come out easier.

He couldn't pull the pin. I'm getting frustrated, so I took the grenade, pulled the pin and carefully wrapped his hand around the handle and told him to throw it, which he did.

About 2 feet in front of us.

I shoved him backwards as hard as I could and dove up the beach. Boom!

Thank God for a few inches of water. No one hurt. Lots of dead fish in the water. Put 'em on the grill.

Chaps, stay away from grenades. Richard, stay away from Chaps!

Company C's Best Job

In late October of 1967 it was decided to begin the job of replacing the temporary bridge over the Song Ban Thach River with a permanent bridge. We knew that the extensive use of pilings would be required and thus began some test pile driving. It soon became apparent that standard H-shaped pilings would not work. They simply never hit bottom, nor was there sufficient friction to keep them from sinking deeper under the weight on them. The bottom of the river muck was several hundred feet deep, an impossible depth to try and reach a hard base.

Fluted piling was to be used as it had a greater surface area and thus told be driven to the point where friction alone could hold the loads designed.

The following is from the history of the battalion.

"Company C began one of the battalion's most on 13 March 1968 one of the battalion's most challenging projects in Vietnam, the construction of a 14-span, 840-foot steel stringer bridge where Highway 1 crossed the Song Ban Thach River. The new bridge would replace a French colonial bridge that the Viet Cong had destroyed in 1966. The company began driving 18-inch steel piles on April 22, some to depths as great as 134 feet. It capped the piles on the 13th and final bent on October 20. The company precast 336 reinforced concrete slabs for the bridge decking using its own concrete batch plant and by mid-November it had placed them atop the steel stringers. Major General David Parker, the U.S. Army, Vietnam, Engineer, joined the Phu Yen province chief to dedicate the bridge on 7 December 1968."

The following picture shows the multiple types of float and fixed bridging that was originally used to replace the French Eiffel bridge over the river, which had been destroyed. The new permanent bridge built by Company C is shown as well. That bridge is still in use today.

Chapter 5 - Phu Hiep (Nov - Jan)

In late October, or early November, I told the battalion commander, LTC MacDonald, that my six months as a company commander were long past, I was worn out and needed to be replaced. He said that as soon as we could find a replacement, I could move up to the S-3 shop as an assistant operations officer. I'd already checked the roster of incoming replacements before making my speech. I told MacDonald that CPT Joe Larremore was due in within a few days, that I knew him, and that he would make a great commander for Company C. Surprisingly, MacDonald agreed that would be okay and that I could make the move as soon as the company could be formally turned over.

Apparently the colonel was still thinking about that other U.S. Army, the one that was not in Vietnam where things take forever to get done. So, when Joe arrived I gave him a quick tour of the unit, introduced the officers and senior NCO's, and briefed him on our mission and the tactical situation in our area. Did he have any questions? No.

All that took about two hours and then I got a ride back to battalion headquarters and told MacDonald that he had a new assistant operations officer. I'm not sure he appreciated the rapid turnover, but it worked out just fine.

Ken Jobe, who had moved to the 3-shop on 5 August, and I were enjoying our work, sort of doing a lot of what we wanted to. We both now agreed that the top 3 officers in the battalion were a bit unsure of how to handle two captains who knew a great deal about their battalion, perhaps too much. The commander was LTC MacDonald, the executive officer was MAJ Tener and the S-3 was MAJ Devereaux. All three were West Point graduates and let us ROTC types know it.

Majors Tener and Devereaux arrived at the same time, but Tener was slightly senior, so he went to the XO spot vacated by MAJ Maturo's rotation. This was unfortunate because the two FNG should have swapped jobs. Devereaux was a paperwork guy who would have been much better suited for the administrative functions of the executive officer. Tener was a better engineer, in my opinion, and should have been the operations officer. But that was not to be.

As previously mentioned, there was a daily meeting to allocate resources, primarily equipment, for the next day's work. But things often got confusing the next day because equipment kept getting moved around, sometimes doing nothing but going from one task to another all day long. The guilty person was usually MAJ Tener. He would visit jobs and decide that a grader, for instance, could better be used on another project, so he would mess up the day's plan. His job did not include this authority and it was a sore point among subordinates on the staff and in the line companies.

Asphalt Truck Fire: 11/24/1967

A terrible accident occurred while SP4 Hector Lopez Ruiz of A Co. was cleaning an asphalt distributor truck. The vehicle burst into flames and, despite the efforts of several men, PFC Lopez suffered fatal burns. He was flown to a military hospital in Japan and died there. He was the sixth soldier from the 577th to die in the Vietnam War.

A Dumped Truck

CPT Jobe was leading the daily road clearing mission along the access road between our base camp and QL-1 when the dump truck following his jeep set off a homemade mine and blew up. I went out there as part of the Quick Reaction Force, though there wasn't much to do. Here's what the truck looked like:

Fortunately, the explosives were offset from the detonator and went off right under the engine. The driver and shotgun were not seriously hurt, though beaten up and both had blown eardrums. They were taken to the 91st Evac. I heard a few days later that they had been awarded Purple Hearts with the hospital staff processing the paperwork. But a guy in the motor pool wondered why he got a Purple Heart when nothing happened to him. Turns out one of the guys in the truck had been wearing his shirt. SNAFU. The First Sergeant got it straightened out, of course.

The mine was apparently intended for one of the transportation company trucks which had a reputation for speeding through the nearby village. And, reportedly, the day before a transportation truck ran over a small girl from that village. Charlie got even, but blew up the wrong unit's truck.

Gee, what an interesting hole that mine left. Lets all look at it.

Bridge Truck Recovery - Route 7B

As previously noted, the 173rd had dumped a brand new truck and its cargo of M4T6 bridging into a canal enroute to Cung Son.

Some time later, I think I was in the S-3 shop at the time, I was tasked to go recover the truck. The 173rd was to provide security. A young airborne infantry lieutenant came over to discuss the situation. He told me that we would move at the pace his men could walk.

Really?

I said that the rough terrain crane we were going to use could move a max of 18 mph. That was going to be our speed.

Mister lieutenant told me that he was the tactical commander and we would do it his way. Now, you do recall that I was a captain at the time? Let's see, a second lieutenant is outranked by a first lieutenant, who is outranked by a captain. Me captain. Yup, that made me the boss of all things tactical and otherwise for this little trip. But, being a fair man, I told him he could go command all the tacticals he wanted to, but not to get in front of that crane or he'd get run over.

We used the crane and a wrecker to extract the truck. The wrecker was driven into the rice paddy to pull from the side, while the crane did the heavy lifting. Once we got the truck out, the crane dragged the wrecker out of the muck. The flat was fixed and the wrecker towed the truck.

And, once again, in and out fast, no problems. At 18 mph.

Counter Ambush

In the same area of QL-1 that CPT Jobe had earlier avoided being ambushed, LT Willard Sudduth recalls his platoon being called in off QL-1 one day and being told to gather up about a dozen of his platoon who were in the immediate area. When they got back to Company C they were quickly loaded up with extra ammo, a couple of M60's, and grenades.

He was directed to go to the low, northernmost hill on the West side of QL-1 not far north of where the road started to climb into the hills around Vung Ro Bay and set up a defensive position atop that hill.

After loading everyone into his jeep and 3/4 ton truck they drove off as fast as we could. They got the vehicles about halfway up the hill and humped their gear to the top of the hill, about another 50 to 100 feet up.

When they got to the top, he recalled it looked like it had been used before because it had been flattened somewhat, but he could not determine if it had been within that decade, century, or millennium. Although it looked like a relatively safe location, it would be a real stretch to call it any sort of a fortification.

He set up a defensive perimeter according to his best recollection of my ROTC and Officer Basic Course training and some welcomed suggestions from the troops. There they waited.....and waited..... and waited.....for about half a day.

Nothing ever happened and they were finally called back to camp and had the extra 'toys' taken away. So it all was a non-event for which he says he is extremely thankful.

Monkey Attack

This story takes place at Duc Trong in 1970, but I thought it so funny that it had to be included. It was written by Roger Bunton who was SP-5 in Company B.

"It was about January 1970 when we were sent out to replace decking on a bridge on the highway going from B Company to the battalion at Duc Trong. Our work crew consisted of four Vietnamese civilians and two soldiers, myself and the other soldier I believe had a last name of Rodgers.

We had been working about an hour on a sunny, rather mild day when one of the civilians pointed down the dry riverbed we were working over and yelled "monkey meat." He repeated it a couple of times until we spotted the monkeys coming toward us in the riverbed out from the forest.

Rodgers and I opened fire on the monkeys and within a few seconds we were fired on from the direction of those monkeys. My first thought was monkeys don't shoot guns and we ducked for cover.

We peered over the railing and started to return fire and it was then we realized that the Viet Cong had been sneaking up on us and had spooked the monkeys to run ahead of them. When we fired on those monkeys the Viet Cong thought we were shooting at them and began returning fire at us. We, in essence, ambushed the Viet Cong who were planning on ambushing us by shooting at the monkeys.

As we were returning fire, I cranked up the PRC 25 and called the artillery base camp next door to our compound, gave them our coordinates and they sent several 155mm rounds into that riverbed area where the Cong were positioned. Needless to say that was a very short firefight once the artillery started landing.

We did manage to score some monkey meat for our civilian workers and that riverbed was a bit deeper in a few spots. We did not find any Viet Cong bodies but located plenty of blood sign, not knowing which was human or animal.

We were visited by an S-3 captain a few hours later and were debriefed by him. When we got back in to our compound we were again debriefed by our Captain and 1st Sgt. What a day and we did not get to come in any earlier just because of a little ole firefight. Needless to say, we downed a few beers that night. I think about that experience anytime I see any kind of monkey."

QRF Again

Early one morning I got a call that there were artillery rounds that had hit QL-1 just off the access road. Take the QRF and check it out.

We got out there and found 3 holes in the asphalt. They seemed about 5-6 inches wide and fairly deep. No idea if there were live rounds in the ground, or what? Maybe a booby trap? Dunno. Dig, but carefully.

About 2 feet into the ground someone from Sub-Area Command tells me a convoy of bombs is coming up the road, so finish up.

Huh, finish up? You dig this hole, man, I'll watch.

Right. I knew they could not stop, or even slow the convoy, so we worked as fast as we could. And after another couple of feet, I saw the ass end of an illumination round that had impacted the road. Fill up the holes, guys, leave 'em in the ground. No danger.

Later on we learned that a Navy cruiser had fired some 5-inch illumination rounds and that was what we found. Fun times on QL-1.

Care Packages

As Christmas 1967 approached the CARE Packages started arriving from home. No, not just family, people all over the country. Most were addressed as "To: A Soldier in Vietnam." The Army postal service spread them out to all units in-country, and they in turn made sure everyone got something.

I remember the S-3 shop receiving a china crate, one of those large cardboard barrels used for moving. It was full of all sorts of goodies, all packed in popcorn to prevent breakage. There was a lot more in there than the few of us could eat, but eat we did, including every last piece of popcorn.

I was really surprised and sorta shocked when I got a newspaper clipping from my wife which had been in the Asheville Citizen-Times. It said that a young couple, about age 24, had adopted me! Really! There was a very nice story about how they felt soldiers in Vietnam were not appreciated, so they found my name in some local source and learned I was a participant in the Southeast Asian War Games. As a measure of appreciation, they had a semi-formal (not so legal) adoption ceremony. Damned nice.

Last Days Before DEROS

Ken and I both had our orders to go home in just 3 days, but both of us had the worst day of our tour at that time.

U.S. Artillery had broken a canal dike and rice paddies were flooding. Since this was out in real indian country, Company D D, 16th Armor, which was part of the 173rd , sent several APCs out to investigate. Ken Jobe was along to determine the best way to fix the damaged dike. The NVA didn't appreciate having this task force out in their area of operations and they heavily attacked with B40 rockets and RPGs. There were quite a few U.S. WIA, including nearly everyone in the track Ken was in. Miraculously, he escaped injury and returned to Phu Hiep unharmed.

On that same day I went on an airborne reconnaissance of route TL-6B and TL-2D since I was familiar with the area. The 95th Regiment was active in the area and the condition of the roads and bridges needed to be reviewed. An infantry lieutenant from the 173rd went with me. We flew in a slick Huey.

Things appeared quiet along TL-6B, but I wanted to check out one of the bridges. The pilot was going to drop us off and then move up to a safe altitude. We'd pop smoke when ready to be picked up.

I grabbed a smoke grenade, the only one on the chopper, and noticed the color was red, which normally meant things were too hot for a helicopter to land. I pointed out the color to the crew chief, who assured me they would come back for us. Hopefully.

The lieutenant and I were underneath the bridge examining the structure when we saw a squad of NVA walking down the road. The two of us obviously were no match for 6 or 7 NVA, so we hid as best we could under the bridge, facing each way in case one of the enemy soldiers came visiting. Fortunately, they kept on walking. We waited until they were out of site and then came out and popped smoke to be picked up.

The next part of the recon was TL-2D from Dong Tre back to TL-6B. This area was far more dangerous than the first part of at the trip, so the pilot was flying at about 100 feet elevation and 100 knots. In order to be able to both see well and make notes at the same time, I made use of the only place you could stick your head out of a Huey and not be beaten by the slipstream. This was right at the front bottom corner of either door opening. The only problem was that you could not be strapped in while lying on the floor. I told the lieutenant to strap in tight and hold onto the back of my harness as tight as he could.

I stuck my head out and was taking notes of the road condition and any likely ambush sites nearby. All went well until we rounded a curve in the road and flew right over an NVA company. Since we were so low, they had not heard us coming and I don't know who was more shocked, them, or us.

Anyway, the young warrant officer pilot immediately pulled pitch and turned off to the right and, as we started to climb, he flew right into the top of a large stand of bamboo. As we crashed through, a bamboo section caught my left arm right in the crook of the elbow and jerked me completely out of the chopper. It was only a few seconds, but it seemed forever as the lieutenant held me by just one harness strap with one hand. I managed to wrap a leg around the landing strut and clawed my way back into the aircraft and then hugged my savior. My only injuries were some bruises and a very sore shoulder. The rest of the recon was uneventful.

Ken and I arrived back at headquarters about the same time and made our reports. MAJ Devereaux started to give us plans for the next day and we both declined to go on any other mission the next day. He understood.

The 35th Group Commander offered us his helicopter for the trip down to the 22^d Replacement Depot at Cam Rahn Bay. We both refused, preferring to ride on the "milk run" C-130 that had 4 engines vs. just one.

The World At Last

After a day at the depot, our "freedom bird" arrived on 10 January 1968 and we boarded with the same feeling of disbelief that I think almost every Vet who returned from Nam has felt.

It was somewhat unique that Ken and I had arrived in Vietnam on the same day, both been company commanders and staff officers in the same battalion, had left on the same day, and had sat side by side on the return trip. The next assignment for both of us was the Engineer Officer Career Course at Fort Belvoir, VA.

We landed back in the world, I think at Oakland, but it didn't matter. After clearing through the processing center we decided we needed a really good meal. We were wearing the same khaki uniforms we had gone over in, quite wrinkled now and probably a bit moldy and ripe. So, when we got to our classy restaurant, they seated us in a back corner away from the real clientele.

We ordered a great meal and afterwards found a barber shop that was still open, had a shoeshine, shave and haircut. While my hair was being cut, I had a thought and suggested to Ken that since we had been back in the states for several hours, perhaps we should call our wives. We did.

A few days later, the battles of Tet 1968 began. Our beloved battalion was hit hard, as was the 91st Evacuation Hospital. I still feel lucky that I missed that time for I am quite sure I would not have survived.

The Sacred Maps

The northern part of the battalion operation area in, which included Cung Son, was covered by several 1:50,000 scale maps. We had just two of each one and couldn't seem to get any more. Stupid. Anyway, the map sets were put on a backing and covered with clear acetate. If you needed one, you had to sign for it and promise not to mess it up. Really.

When I rotated home, I attended the Engineer Officer Career Course at Fort Belvoir, something that should have been done before becoming a company commander. After three commands, they sure weren't gonna give me any more, but for my money, it was the best damn job in the entire Army and I'd have done it forever.

Several months into the course, we had a tactics class taught by a Marine major. The "problem" for which we had to devise a solution was how to get a convoy down the very enemy infested route Route 7B from Tuy Hoa to the special forces camp at Cung Son. There were several officers who had recently returned from the 577th. We presented a simple solution that the major just could not believe. What was it?

Don't tell your headquarters or other units that you were going, and then get in and get out as fast as possible using airlifted mine sweep teams to clear the road. Keep aviation support and artillery on call.

The proven logic had worked many times because it took the bad guys some time to get their act together. As long as we were faster, there was never a problem.

By the way, those maps I mentioned? The storage room for that class had hundreds of them in it! There was only one solution. During the lunch break, we took nearly all of them and had them sent to the good old 577th as fast as they could get there!

Final Thoughts

I knew we'd lost the war one night when I was in our nice comfy Officer's Club, having a drink and watching my alma mater, NC State, in the Liberty Bowl on Armed Forces Vietnam Television. I could hear the choppers come in to refuel, rearm and take off again from the airfield, plus a few pot shots being fired on the perimeter. I wonder how things would have gone if so much effort had not been wasted on things like television stations, permanent buildings in Saigon and elsewhere, not even mentioning the absolutely huge amount of engineer resources spent on building SEA huts. We had lots of perfectly good tents which had worked just fine earlier. As soon as we moved under tin roofs, the amount of power required to service the battalion increased sixfold. And this was true all over the country. You'd think we were stateside.

The reason for the war is sometimes foggy, but probably the best answer is the so-called Domino Theory in which if any Southeast Asia nation fell to communism, it would start the fall of all, or most, of the others. Obviously, this was proven false, but there was real concern about it at the time. The French had been defeated in 1954 and Ho Chi Minh's army, led by General Vo Nguyen Giap, was infiltrating into the southern half of the country even as it was being partitioned at the end of the war.

General Westmoreland's war of attrition was not going anywhere and the politicos in Washington did not have the balls to strike the enemy where we really needed to. Yes, we were bombing around Hanoi and Haiphong, but not in those cities. In my opinion, the war could have been won in short order had we done that and also destroyed the Red River dikes, flooding much of North Vietnam. Huge numbers of people would have died, but over 2,000,000 on both sides died in South Vietnam.

In 1966, John McNaughton, Secretary of Defense for International Security Affairs, proposed the destruction of the Red River Valley dams and dikes in order to flood rice paddies, disrupt the North Vietnamese food supply, and leverage Hanoi during negotiations; then Secretary of Defense Robert McNamara, however, rejected the idea. He preferred to micro-manage the disaster.

In his book printed shortly before his death, *McNamara admitted that in 1965 he knew we could not win in Vietnam.* U.S. deaths at that point were approximately 5,000. McNamara was Secretary of Defense from 1961 to 1967 under both presidents Kennedy and Johnson. When McNamara left office, 15,979 Americans had been killed in Vietnam; by the time the United States left Vietnam, the number stood at 58,282. This was obviously McNamara's war as he was the early architect who took us into a quagmire in which our country sank ever deeper, and from which we finally ran away. May he rot in hell.

Yes, the South Vietnamese governments were totally corrupt but the U.S. attempts to democratize and nation build were foolhardy. We got ourselves into a war we did not wish to win in a country that did not like us. Perhaps our leaders were afraid of China and Russia. No one knows for sure.

But one thing is painfully true — this was an American war. If we had to be there, we should have trained the ARVN and let them do the

149

fighting for their own country, with our support. Instead, we did most of the fighting for them. Respect was lost all around.

Sounds just like a few other places our military has been in over the past 15 years.

As the years go by, I have decided that we have gained nothing from any war we have been involved in since World War II. I am not opposed to war if it is a matter of national survival, but if that is the case, you play to win, otherwise you lose. We lost in Vietnam in a most disgraceful and shameful way. We learned very little from that war and followed the same course in Iraq and Afghanistan, another two wars we had no business being in.

Today we are fighting ISIS and Assad. We are allied with both Shia and Sunni arabs. These two branches of Islam have been at each others throats for fourteen centuries, but that doesn't explain all the political, economic, and geopolitical factors involved in these conflicts. It has, however, become one prism through which to understand the underlying tensions. Two countries that compete for the leadership of Islam, Sunni Saudi Arabia and Shia Iran, have used the sectarian divide to further their ambitions.

The point of this is that the United States cannot and will not settle anything between these two religious sects. They can only do it themselves and we have no business aligning with either group. Anything we do merely increases the hatred for us from one side or the other.

But, going back to Vietnam, it would not be right if I didn't express my thoughts about the enemy we confronted in Phu Yen province. The Viet Cong were dedicated to their cause and fought well, though they were generally not well equipped. They took time to get their act together which served to our benefit as engineers who, for the most part, were operating on our own without infantry support.

The North Vietnamese Army was another story. The principal NVA element in Phu Yen was the 95th Regiment. These men and women were tough, highly motivated and professional. They were well equipped, though not nearly as mobile as their helicopter borne opponents. I had, and still have, great respect for their soldiers and leaders. Besides, they won...

Today the Socialist Republic of Vietnam is a vibrant nation which is on the way to being a major trading partner and probably an eventual ally of the United States.

Lastly, though the reader may disagree with some of the comments made herein, these things are forever true:

1. The year 1967 was the most momentous, interesting and meaningful year of my life. I could not be more proud of the men who served under my command, other members of the 577th Engineer Battalion (Construction), as well as with other units we worked with.

2. I am most thankful than none of the men under my command were killed or wounded.

3. Although I have been often been critical of the Army, it was, and is, the world's most powerful and wonderful entity.

4. Fellow Veterans, I salute you all.

Alachua, FL
March 2016

Appendix A - Those Who Fell

NAME	RAN MOS	UNIT	DATE	CATEGORY
HEINZ, DONALD E	PFC 62E	C CO 577 ENG BN	07/05/67	ACCIDENT
PACE, DANNY WAYNE	PVT 62W	C CO 577 ENG BN	07/29/67	HOMICIDE
CAREW, FARRELL RICHARD	SGT	553 ENG CO (FB)	08/30/67	KIA
HOOPER, JULIAN R	MSG	553 ENG CO (FB)	08/30/67	KIA
RANKIN, EDWARD LEE	PFC 623	553 ENG CO (FB)	08/30/67	KIA
RUIZ, HECTOR LOPEZ	SP4	A CO 577 ENG BN	11/24/67	ACCIDENT
BINGMAN, RONALD HOWARD	SSG 62H	C CO 577 ENG BN	04/09/68	HOMICIDE
YOUNG, CALVIN EDWARD	SSG 51H	B CO 577 ENG BN	11/30/68	KIA
BEACHAM ,WARREN LEE	CPL 62L	D CO 577 ENG BN	03/02/69	KIA
JOHNSON, CALVIN	SP5 62B	A CO 577 ENG BN	03/10/69	ACCIDENT
REID, AUBREY ARCHIE JR	PFC 51B	A CO 577 ENG BN	04/18/69	KIA
WHEELER, OSCAR LEE	PFC 51A	C CO 577 ENG BN	05/09/69	ACCIDENT
VAUGHAN, RAYMOND WALTER	SP4 62E	B CO 577 ENG BN	09/02/69	ACCIDENT
LA GRAY, ERNEST JAMES	PVT 12B	B CO 577 ENG BN	11/14/69	KIA
METCALF, RICHARD LOUIS	SP4 62E	A CO 577 ENG BN	01/21/70	ACCIDENT
BOOTH, WILLIAM DOUGLAS	CPT 51331	HHC, ENG CMD	05/12/70	KIA
HAGER, THOMAS GARY	PFC 62M	D CO 577 ENG BN	06/17/70	ACCIDENT
NICODEMUS, WILLIAM DEO	SP4 62E	B CO 577 ENG BN	01/26/71	ACCIDENT
BOUCHARD, WILLIAM J	PVT 51B	C CO 577 ENG BN	08/28/71	ACCIDENT
JOHNSON, HARVEY DOUGLAS	SP5	B CO 577 ENG BN	11/04/71	HOMICIDE
TEMPLETON, DAVID LEE	SP4	C CO 577 ENG BN	12/27/71	ACCIDENT

Rest In Peace My Brothers

Appendix B - Heraldry

(From The Institute of Heraldry)

Description/Blazon

A Silver color metal and enamel device 1 1/8 inches (2.86 cm) in height overall consisting of a shield blazoned: Per fess Argent and Gules in chief a spur gear, in base a shovel fesswise, handle to sinister, counterchanged. Attached below the shield a Silver scroll inscribed "AGENDO GNAVITER" in Red letters.

Symbolism

In the scarlet and white of the Engineer Corps, the functions of the organization are aptly illustrated in the gear and shovel, both symbolizing the mechanical and hand tools necessary in the performance of their work.

Background

The distinctive unit insignia was originally approved for the 377th Engineer Battalion on 14 October 1942. It was redesignated for the 377th Engineer General Service Regiment on 15 September 1943. The insignia was redesignated for the 577th Engineer Battalion (Construction) on 8 March 1955.

Coat of Arms

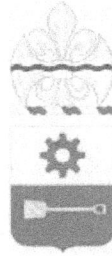

Description/Blazon

Shield

Per fess Argent and Gules in chief a spur gear, in base a shovel fesswise, handle to sinister, counterchanged.

Crest

On a wreath of the colors Argent and Gules, a fleur-de-lis and a double axe head per cross of the first charged with a wavy bar fesswise Azure.

Motto

AGENDO GNAVITER (By Doing Diligently).

Symbolism

Shield

In the scarlet and white of the Engineer Corps, the functions of the organization are aptly illustrated in the gear and shovel, both symbolizing the mechanical and hand tools necessary in the performance of their work.

Crest

The fleur-de-lis is used to symbolize France, and the double axe head is placed to represent the unit's action across her border. The wavy blue bar is used to symbolize the Rhineland. The two blades of the axe refer to the two campaign honors awarded the unit during World War II.

Background

The coat of arms was originally approved for the 377th Engineer Battalion, Organized Reserve on 14 October 1942. It was redesignated for the 377th Engineer General Service Regiment on 15 September 1943. It was redesignated for the 577th Engineer Battalion (Construction) and amended by deletion of the Organized Reserve crest on 8 March 1955. The coat of arms was amended to add a crest on 15 February 1967.

Iron Soldiers in Vietnam

Appendix C - History

"Iron Soldiers"

AGENDO GNAVITER

By Charles Hendricks
Office of History
U.S. Army Corps of Engineers
30 June 1987

As the United States Army grew rapidly in the months after the nation entered World War II, the War Department issued orders on 24 April 1942 for the organization of nine additional engineer units. Four of those units, including the 377th Engineer Battalion (Separate), the antecedent of today's 577th Engineer Battalion, were to consist of black enlisted personnel in an army that remained segregated on racial lines. Second Army activated the 377th on 15 July 1942 at Camp Pickett, a newly opened installation located near Blackstone in Southside Virginia. The battalion's first commander was Lieutenant Colonel Henry G. Douglas, a 1927 West Point graduate, and its initial cadre of enlisted men came from the 383rd Engineer Battalion (Separate), which had been activated just four months earlier.

The battalion trained at Camp Pickett until 1 April 1943, when it moved by rail to fort Knox, Kentucky, on orders from Lieutenant General Leslie McNair, commander of Army Ground Forces. There it was assigned to Armored Force, an organization which, under the command of Lieutenant General Jacob Devers, controlled the training of virtually all armored units in the United States. It remained with the armored command for only four months, however. On 2 August 1943, a day after its relief from that assignment, the battalion was reorganized and redesignated as the 377th Engineer General Service Regiment. The battalion's commander at Fort Knox, Major Charles Flournoy, assumed initial command of the regiment. The engineer general service regiment, with a strength of 52 officers, 3 warrant officers, and 1,267 enlisted men, was only slightly larger than the separate battalion's strength of 33 officers, 1 warrant officer, and 1,084 enlisted men, but the regiment's additional heavy equipment made the new organization much more Productive and efficient. The Corps of Engineers had in February 1943 called the engineer separate battalions "a relic of 1917" and had argued that their members, whether black or white, could provide the trained machinery operators and other specialists required for general service regiments. The reorganization of the 377th was part of a general phase-out of engineer separate battalions which followed this recommendation.

The 377th now quickly completed its stateside training at Fort Knox. On 14 October 1943 it received a new commander, Colonel Amos T. Akerman, a 1925 Military Academy graduate and Georgia native who would lead the regiment until the end of the war. On November 1, the new commander gave the slightly over-strength unit an efficiency rating of excellent. The unit moved to Camp Shanks, New York, in mid-November, and on 23 November 1943 it sailed from New York for England aboard the Queen Elizabeth.

Upon its arrival in Great Britain at the end of November 1943, the 377th Engineer General Service Regiment went immediately to county Devon in southwestern England, where for four months it engaged in the construction of large camps for the American troops that would be debarking for France. Elements of the regiment were dispersed around Devon to permit them to work more conveniently on their assigned Projects. When this work ended in the spring, the regiment moved farther west to Chacewater Camp near Truro in Cornwall and there engaged in basic and specialist training. It was alerted at the end of April for movement to the continent.

The regiment moved to France in late July, landing on Utah Beach on the last day of the month. Its 1st Battalion helped construct a 20,000-man rest camp at Carteret and Barneville-surMer, on the West coast of the Cotentin Peninsula. about 20 miles south of Cherbourg. It also removed enemy mines from a five-mile stretch of coast south of Carteret, suffering the loss of one killed and five wounded in the operation. The regiment moved south and east to near Le Mans in mid-August, where it received a quick initiation in railroad repair work. Its 2d Battalion assisted the 368th Engineer General Service Regiment in rehabilitating about 20 miles of double-track rail line from Le Mans northwest to Sille-le-Guillaume in an area held by Germans less than a week before. Following immediately behind the British and American forces that cleared the western Part of the Falaise pocket on 16-18 August, the regiment then rehabilitated the 20 miles of double-track rail line from Flers east to Ecouche. utilizing 1,000 German prisoners in this work.

The regiment and its prisoner-cf-war laborers moved east of Paris at the beginning of September with enough railcars to transport its entire strength. Here it restored more than 100 miles of track between Laon, located some 65 miles northeast of Paris, and Conflans, situated 14 miles west of embattled Metz and 160 miles east of Paris. The work included clearing a 3,200-foot tunnel and constructing a single-track bridge across the Longeau River. This rail line, which passed through the French cities of Reims and Verdun, would become an important supply channel for General Patton's Third Army. After completing this task at the end of September, the regiment was assigned to guard and consolidate captured engineer equipment at many points in France, Belgium, and Luxembourg.

The 377th was reassigned in early November 1944 to the Continental Advance Section, the logistical organization that had supported Seventh Army's landing at Marseilles in mid-September and now had its headquarters at Dijon in Burgundy. The companies of the 377th began a number of construction Projects in mid-November in the region between Dijon and Nancy. They improved the 2,000-bed general hospitals at Mirecourt and Vittel and the 500-bed station hospital at Epinal, and they built three ordnance shops--an automotive shop at Langres, an armament repair shop at Gray, and an armament maintenance shop at Chaumont. The facilities occupied in mid-October by the 21st General Hospital on an 864-acre estate at Mirecourt, once owned by a marquis, posed particular challenges. The hospital was installed in an unfinished neuropsychiatric hospital that the French government had begun in 1934. French workers had sabotaged the complicated water and steam heating system of the hospital's 23 buildings to prevent their use by the Germans, but the American engineers and hospital staff quickly put them back into operation in 1944. The hospital was overcrowded in November 1944-January 1945, and as the engineers made each building habitable, it was filled with patients. The 377th erected an additional 50 prefabricated hospital ward buildings in January 1945, increasing the hospital's capacity to 4,000 patients.

The regiment remained in and near Lorraine until the Allied victory in Europe. On 25 February 1945 in was assigned, with other units in the area, to the Burgundy District, a new base section organization. The European theater Communications Zone headquarters removed that district, with the 377th under it, from the Continental Advance Section and placed it under the Oise Section on 21 March. Through these administrative changes, the regiment continued to develop the hospitals at Mirecourt and Vittel, but as it finished its other assignments several of its companies began operating quarries and maintaining roads in the upper Marne Valley.

General Eisenhower's European theater headquarters in early June ordered the 377th Engineer General Service Regiment to prepare to move to the Southwest Pacific theater. The unit moved to the nearby assembly area at Camp Boston on 21 June and then to the staging area for the port of Marseilles at the end of August. By then, however, the Americans' use of atomic weapons had brought Japan to its knees, so the European theater command was able to retain the regiment. It shipped the regiment to Nurnberg, Germany, in mid-September. Working at several localities in northern Bavaria, the 377th rehabilitated an army general hospital in Nurnberg, began constructing new buildings for a similar hospital in Bayreuth and roads at two ammunition dumps at Bamberg, and relocated 1,500 feet of pipeline in the Nurnberg area. It redeployed to France once more at the beginning of December and sailed from Antwerp on the Sedalia Victory on 20 December 1945. Arriving at Hampton Roads, Virginia, on 3 January 1946, the regiment was deactivated the same day at Camp Patrick Henry, Virginia.

The Army did not activate the 377th Engineer General Service Regiment during the Korean War. In February 1954, however, it redesignated the unit as the 577th Engineer Battalion and allotted it to the Regular Army, simultaneously disbanding the regiment's first battalion headquarters and its entire second battalion. The 577th Engineer Battalion was then activated on 25 August 1954 at Fort Benning, Georgia, as an engineer construction Battalion. It served there for the next 12 years, during which time it undertook so many construction projects at that installation that it coined for itself the slogan. "We Build Fort Benning." Noteworthy among its projects during these years were the construction or expansion of Fryar Field and Dekkar Air Strip and the Kelley BiLl and Todd Field Heliports, and the rehabilitation of Buckner Range. The battalion also worked on projects at Fort Jackson South Carolina, the Dahlonega Ranger Camp in Georgia, and Fort McClellan, Alabama.

During the period 1955-1963 the 577th was attached to the 151st Engineer Group at Fort Benning. Members of the battalion participated in October 1961 in combat readiness demonstrations for President John Kennedy at Fort Bragg, North Carolina, for which the participants were congratulated by the president. During the same year the entire battalion received a course in controlling riots and civil disturbances, and in the autumn of, 1962, members of the 577th helped maintain order at the University of Mississippi as it admitted its first black student. Throughout this period, the battalion was often understrength, and it had particular difficulty in obtaining enough construction machine operators, maintenance personnel, and electricians.

> ADDED NOTE: During the Cuban Crisis, without any advance notice, the 577th deployed 3 reinforced Engineer General Construction Platoons from a RVN tactical scenario during a FTX in the Benning woods to Florida [Eglin AFB, Homestead AFB and a third location near Miami]. The platoons prepared camps for the 82nd and 101 Airborne Infantry Divisions to parachute into Cuba. Once completed, the platoons provided direct support to base facility engineering.

The battalion was first alerted for deployment to Southeast Asia in October 1965. With its personnel continually tapped for other units deploying to Vietnam, the 577th remained well understrength until January 1966, when 350 enlisted men joined the unit for basic and then advanced training. The unit conducted this training despite a substantial shortage of officers that persisted well into the spring. The bulk of the unit sailed from Oakland Army Terminal on 7 July 1966 and arrived at Cam Rahn Bay, Vietnam, at the end of that month. Even though the first U.S. Army engineer units in Vietnam had landed at Cam Rahn Bay just 13 months earlier, a substantial port and military base had already been established there. Assigned to the 45th construction at Dong Ba Thin, just west of the bay, where a military airfield had been built by Company C of the 65th Engineer Battalion and the 20th Engineer Battalion over the previous year. After filling a tidal swamp to an elevation of six feet, the 577th built barracks, sanitary and recreational facilities, mess halls, and administrative offices on concrete floor pads in three cantonment areas at Dong Ba Thin. During October 1966 Company D of the battalion built six two-story barracks for a replacement depot across the bay at Cam Ranh Bay.

Some elements of the battalion worked on assignments at some distance from Dong Ba Thin. In September and October 1966 Company B replaced the stringers and decking on a 725-foot bridge at Dien Khanh, west of Nha Trang, removing the M4T6 aluminum balk decking for tactical use elsewhere and increasing the bridge's capacity to 35 tons. Company C of the 577th went by plane & truck to Long Binh near Saigon immediately upon its arrival in Vietnam, and there it was attached to the 46th Engineer Battalion. On this detached service, the company supported the 46th's construction of a huge ammunition depot at Long Binh, and itself constructed housing primarily for women troops at Tan Son Nhut and Long Binh and built and maintained roads in the area. On 22 January 1967 the company moved by convoy and landing craft to My Tho in the Mekong Company D, where it built two Bailey bridges to Don Tam, opening it to heavy traffic. The company then began construction at Don Tam of a 7,500-man base camp for a brigade of the 9th Infantry Division.

The 577th Engineer Battalion moved to Tuy Hoa, located some 100 miles up the coast from Dong Ba Thin, during 11-19 November 1966. Switching positions with the 14th Engineer Battalion, the 577th traveled uneventfully in four convoys of 60 to 100 vehicles each up coastal Highway 1, a route long dominated by the Viet Cong. Company D built a 3500 foot runway for C-130 aircraft and a heliport for Chinook aircraft and a 400-bed evacuation hospital at Tuy Hoa and maintained the 17 miles of Highway 1 from that town to Port Lane on Vung Ro Bay. Company A operated an aggregate quarry and an asphalt Plant near Tuy Hoa. Company B meanwhile helped a Private contractor to install a Prefabricated DeLong Pier at Port Lane, moving some 30,000 cubic Yards of rock fill to construct a causeway to the Pier. The company drew some of this rock from a mile-long connecting road that it blasted out along a cliff overlookinq the bay to another section of the port that it would develop. After completing the causeway in late January 1967, the company worked on other projects at Port Lane, including a 500-man cantonment, petroleum tanks and retail facilities and 40,000 square Yards of rock hardstands for off-loading.

Soon after the 69th engineer Battalion arrived in Vietnam at the beginning of May 1967, the personnel and equipment of Company C of the 577th , then working at Dong Tam in the Company D, were transferred to Company B of the 69th, The personnel and equipment that had arrived in Vietnam as Company B of the 69th were sent to Tuy Hoa, and on 24, May 1967 they were transferred into Company C of the 577th. In that way, the 577th was reunified. A month later Company C deployed to Dong Tre in the hills northwest of Tuy Hoa,where in July it built an airfield with an all-weather. 2,800-foot runway for C-123 cargo planes. The company also upgraded 7 miles of Route 2D from Dong Tre to Highway 1 north of Tuy Hoa. Meanwhile during May and June 1967, Company D built at Phu Hiep, on the coast just south of Tuy Hoa, a 3,500-foot runway and parallel taxiway together with a hardstand parking apron. This Project involved grading the sand. mixing it with soil cement, sealing the mixture with an asphaltic coat, and laying M8A1 matting for the runway. The battalion completed a 66-pad heliport at Phu Hiep Army Airfield the following spring.

The fall and winter of 1967-1968 was a difficult period for the 577th Engineer Battalion. Typhoon Freida struck the Tuy Hoa area with 125 mile-per-hour winds on 10 November 1967. It washed away 30 feet of the causeway leading out to the DeLong pier at the Phu Hiep airfield and destroyed two frame maintenance buildings used by the battalion. The unit installed a 45-foot, M-4 fixed span to keep the DeLong pier in operation. The enemy began its Tet offensive on 1 February 1968. The Viet Cong struck the perimeter of the Tuy Hoa cantonment three times by 6 March, wounding 11 members of the 577th , but each time the battalion and supporting units repelled the attackers. After enemy artillery fire destroyed the main irrigation canal of the Hieu Xuong District, the 577th helped Vietnamese citizens to restore it.

Company C began on 13 March 1968 one of the battalion's most challenging projects in Vietnam, the construction of a 14-span, 840-foot steel stringer bridge where Highway 1 crossed the Ban Thach River. The new bridge would replace a French colonial bridge that the Viet Cong had destroyed in 1966. The company began driving 18-inch steel piles on April 22, some to depths as great as 134 feet. It capped the piles on the 13th and final bent on October 20. The company precast 336 reinforced concrete slabs for the bridge decking using its own concrete batch plant, and by mid-November it had placed them atop the steel stringers. Major General David Parker, the U.S. Army, Vietnam, Engineer, joined the Phu Yen province chief to dedicate the bridge on 7 December 1968.

Meanwhile on 10 June 1968, Company B of the battalion began the Vung Ro Mountain section of Highway 1 upgrade. The company blasted over 70,000 cubic yards of earth from the mountain cut and placed 18,000 cubic yards of fill before the end of 1968, improving a road that previously had been little more than a path in places. Company B also improved the access road to the Vung Ro mountain top signal station, widening and leveling a road with grades over 15 percent. After the enemy attacked the cantonment at Vung Ro Bay on 6 June 1968, the unit cleared a 110-yard-wide, 1.7-mile-long swath across the mountainous terrain bounding the camp and built six fighting bunkers and an observation tower. During the first three months of 1969, Company D cleared a 110 yard-wide strip of trees and brush along the 28-mile-long section of road up the Da Rang and Ba valleys from Tuy Hoa to Cung Son. This protected from enemy ambushes on road that had earlier been upgraded to 18-ton capacity by an engineer light equipment company attached to the 577th. Company D used several Rome plows, standard military tractors equipped with special tree cutting blades, supplemented by 2,100 boxes of bangalore torpedoes employed on steep and rocky areas, to clear the 813 acres stripped in this project.

As these projects and the continuing development of the Phu Hiep Airfield reached completion, the battalion was gradually redeployed, by elements, in the first half of 1969 to Don Duong and Duc Trong in the Central Highlands of Vietnam, near Dalat. Company D, however, returned to Dong Ba Thin in March 1969, and there its personnel and equipment were transferred into Company D of the 589th Engineer Battalion. The men who had previously served as Company D, 589th Engineer Battalion, were already at Don Duong, and they then filled Company D of the 577th. Company B of the 577th , which completed the upgrading of Highwav 1 from Tuy Hoa to Vung Ro Bay, was the last to leave Phu Yen Province. The battalion finished this project on 22 May

1969, having completed 19 miles of asphalt pavement through a mountain pass and long stretches of rice paddy, built five major steel stringer bridges, and repaired two other bridges that had been partially destroyed by enemy explosives. When Company B reached upland Tuyen Duc Province on 1 June, other elements of the 577th had begun the development of base camps at Don Duong and Duc Trong, but these were not completed until autumn.

In the highlands, the battalion was assigned the task of upgrading to standards set by the U.S. Military Assistance Command, Vietnam, a total of 91 miles of Highways 11, 20, and 21A (later named Highway 21B) between Di Linh, Dalat, Don Duong, and Song Pha. It would concentrate its efforts on the Portions of those roads that formed part of a critical through route from Saigon to Cam Rahn Bay, bypassing Dalat. On Highway 11 Company D of the 577th built during May-July 1969 a 230-foot triple-single Bailey bridge supported by two timber-crib Piers across the Da Nhim River at Don Duong. It also erected a 70-foot double-single Bailey bridge on Highway 20 near Di Linh to replace one that had failed under excessive loads. Progress on road improvement was generally slow, however, particularly after the monsoon rains arrived in September, bringing 23 inches of rain to Don Duong in that month. A 250-ton-per-hour Cedar Rapids crusher that Company A of the battalion set up in August 1969 operated only briefly that year, due to the collapse of the headwall and rain damage to the haul road from the quarry.

Once the rains had subsided and essential repairs had been made to the roads and bridges in the area, the 577th directed its primary efforts to upgrading Highway 21B, a 16-mile cutoff road between Don Duong and Duc Trong, south of Dalat. Enemy activity continued in this period. The Duc Trong base camp was hit by mortar fire twice in early November and again in April 1970, and on 18 January 1970 the enemy destroyed a disabled D-7E dozer that had to be left overnight at an insecure worksite. Nevertheless, work continued apace, with the laying of base course peaking in January 1970 and paving averaging a steady four miles a month on the road in February, March, and April. By April Highway 21B had advanced enough to allow Companies B and C of the 577th to begin to improve a portion of Highway 20, the major route from the Saigon area to Dalat. During this period Company D of the 577th worked on Highway 11 east of Don Duong, paving some 8 miles of rebuilt roadway.

Highway 21B ran through the Da Nhim valley, and the 577th had to construct new bridges over the many tributaries of the Da Nhim. Companies B and C of the battalion focused on this work during the summer and autumn of 1970. Company D. aided by a substantial group of locally hired civilians, concentrated its efforts on the section of Highway 1 1 between Don Duong and Dong Pha, in which the road descended in a series of switchbacks down the rugged littoral of the Central Highlands toward Phan Rang. Its work included cutting and filling for improved headwalls and the installation of culverts for all the mountain streams. These streams could rise dramatically during the monsoon season. When the rains hit the highlands, the 577th moved its earthmoving equipment to Highway I on the coastal Plain south of Phan Rang, where the rains were less severe. There its equipment operators supported the road-building work of the 589th Engineer Battalion.

After the upgrading of Highway 21B was completed in February 1971, Companies B and C shifted their focus to improving the section of Highway 20 southwest of Duc Trong at the western terminus of Highway 21B. The work on this route had to be limited, however, as the battalion's strength was gradually cut and some of its equipment was transferred to the Vietnamese during the year as part of the American withdrawal of forces from Vietnam. The companies worked on three substantial new bridges on the road and rebuilt and paved six miles of roadway south of the junction with Highway 21B. In September 1971 the battalion turned over its work on Highway 20 to the 61st Engineer Battalion of the Army of the Republic of Vietnam.

Company D continued in 1971 it's work on the rugged stretch of Highway 11 between Don Duong and Song Pha, A roadway failure that had occurred near Duc Me during the previous fall monsoon required cutting 15 feet into the uphill bank and moving 200,000 cubic yards of earth. The company also strengthened switchbacks and widened them to at least 19.6 feet (6 meters) in width. By October 1971, South Vietnamese authorities had accepted 16 miles of improved roadway from the company. Together with the adjoining roadwork on Highway 11 done by the 589th Engineer Battalion, the product was a modern, paved highway from Phan Rang on the coast to Don Duong in the Highlands. As the battalion's service in Vietnam drew to a close, Company B moved down Highway 20 from Duc Trong to Di Linh in August 1971 to support the highway construction efforts of the 815th Engineer Battalion. Tasked to do rough earthwork and sub-grade, the company moved over 100,000 cubic yards of earth from cuts west of Di Linh, strongly impressing its new supervisors. It worked on this project until early December, when the 815th was also ordered to prepare for inactivation.

Company A of the 577th , which had for two years operated the rock crushers and asphalt plant at Don Duong, meanwhile dismantled the site and, in numerous convoys, carried the equipment to the coast for shipment to the United States. During the last three months of its service in Vietnam, the battalion headquarters oversaw the work of separate engineer companies at the Ban Me Thuot and Weigt-Davis work sites, the latter located 25 miles south of Pleiku, as the companies turned those facilities over to Vietnamese engineer units. With the reduction of its forces virtually complete, a color guard from the 577th brought the battalion's colors to Scofield Barracks, Hawaii, at the end of January 1972. The battalion was refilled in Hawaii, and it served as an engineer construction battalion at Schofield Barracks until 11 July 1972, when it was inactivated. Most recently, the battalion was activated on 30 September 1986 at Fort Leonard Wood, Missouri, and assigned to the U.S. Army Training Center Engineer.

During the course of its service the 577th Engineer Battalion Participated in two campaigns in World War II and thirteen campaigns in Vietnam. The Army awarded two meritorious unit commendations to the battalion,the first for its service in the Cam Ranh Bay and Tuy Hoa areas from 2 August 1966 to 1 1 June 1967 and the second for work at Tuy Hoa and Vung Ro Bay from 12 June 1967 to 7 December 1968. Company C of the 577th , which had been attached to the 46th Engineer Battalion upon its arrival in Vietnam, was a co-recipient of the meritorious unit commendation awarded to that battalion for work at Long Binh and Dong Tam from May 1966 to April 1967. Finally, the battalion headquarters element was awarded a civil actions medal by the Republic of Vietnam for the service it Performed in that country between 3 May 1970 and 30 April 1971.

Appendix D - Agent Orange

Agent Orange

The Gift That Keeps On Giving

From Wikipedia

Agent Orange—or Herbicide Orange (HO)—is one of the herbicides and defoliants used by the U.S. military as part of its herbicidal warfare program, Operation Ranch Hand,[1] during the Vietnam War from 1961 to 1971.[2] It was a mixture of equal parts of two herbicides, 2,4,5-T and 2,4-D.

During the late 1940s and 1950s, the U.S. and British collaborated on development of herbicides with potential applications in warfare.

Some of those products were brought to market as herbicides. The British were the first to employ herbicides and defoliants to destroy the crops, bushes, and trees of communist insurgents in Malaya during the Malayan Emergency. These operations laid the groundwork for the subsequent use of Agent Orange and other defoliant formulations by the U.S..[3]

In mid-1961, President Ngo Dinh Diem of South Vietnam asked the United States to conduct aerial herbicide spraying in his country. In August of that year, the South Vietnamese Air Force initiated herbicide operations with American help. But Diem's request launched a policy debate in the White House and the State and Defense Departments.[1] However, U.S. officials considered using it, pointing out that the British had already used herbicides and defoliants during the Malayan Emergency in the 1950s. In November 1961, President John F. Kennedy authorized the start of Operation Ranch Hand, the codename for the U.S. Air Force's herbicide program in Vietnam.

[Ed. Note: The name signifies orange identifying bands that were used on the fifty-five gallon drums the product was shipped in. Other herbicides were also used in Vietnam, and were known by color coded names too, such Agent White, Agent Blue, Agent Purple, Agent Pink and Agent Green were also used.]

Agent Orange was manufactured for the U.S. Department of Defense primarily by Monsanto Corporation and Dow Chemical.[4,6] It was given its name from the color of the orange-striped barrels in which it was shipped, and was by far the most widely used of the so-called "Rainbow Herbicides."[5] The 2,4,5-T used to produce Agent Orange was contaminated with 2,3,7,8-Tetrachlorodibenzodioxin (TCDD), an extremely toxic dioxin compound. In some areas, TCDD concentrations in soil and water were hundreds of times greater than the levels considered safe by the U.S. Environmental Protection Agency.[6,7]

In the absence of specific customary or positive international humanitarian law regarding herbicidal warfare, a draft convention, prepared by a Working Group set up within the Conference of the Committee on Disarmament (CCD), was submitted to the UN General Assembly in 1976. In that same year, the First Committee of the General Assembly decided to send the text of the draft convention to the General Assembly, which adopted Resolution 31/72 on December 10, 1976, with the text of the Convention attached as an annex thereto. The convention, namely the Environmental Modification Convention, was opened for signature and ratification on May 18, 1977, and entered into force in October 5, 1978. The convention prohibits the military or other hostile use of environmental modification techniques having widespread, long-lasting or severe effects. Many states do not regard this as a complete ban on the use of herbicides and defoliants in warfare but it does require case-by-case consideration.[8,9]Although in the Geneva Disarmament Convention of 1978, Article 2(4) Protocol III to the weaponry convention has "The Jungle Exception", which prohibits states from attacking forests or jungles "except if such natural elements are used to cover, conceal or camouflage combatants or military objectives or are military objectives themselves" this voids any protection of any military or civilians from a napalm attack or something like agent Orange and is clear that it was designed to cater to situations like U.S. tactics in Vietnam. This clause has yet to be revised.[10]

This page was last modified on 16 December 2015, at 15:59.

Text is available under the Creative Commons Attribution-ShareAlike License

---

References

1 Buckingham. "The Air Force and Herbicides"

2 Agent Orange Linked To Skin Cancer Risk

3 Bruce Cumings (1998). The Global Politics of Pesticides: Forging Consensus from Conflicting Interests. Earthscan. p. 61.

4 "Agent Orange" entry in Encyclopedia of United States National Security, edited by Richard J. Samuel. SAGE Publications, 2005. ISBN 9781452265353

5 Hay, 1982: p. 151

6 Fawthrop, Tom; "Vietnam's war against Agent Orange", BBC News, June 14, 2004

7 Fawthrop, Tom; "Agent of Suffering", Guardian, February 10, 2008

8 Convention on the Prohibition of the Military or Any Other Hostile Use of Environmental Modification Techniques

9 "Practice Relating to Rule 76. Herbicides." International Committee of the Red Cross. 2013. Retrieved 24 August 2013.

10 Detter, Ingrid.)The Law of War],)Ashgate pub. 2013] pg. 255.

11. IOM, 1994: p. 90

12. Frumkin, 2003: pp.245–255

VA maintains a list of U.S. Navy and Coast Guard ships associated with military service in Vietnam and possible exposure to Agent Orange based on military records. This evolving list helps Veterans who served aboard ships, including "Blue Water Veterans," find out if they may qualify for presumption of herbicide exposure.

Currently there are 344 ships on this list. A veteran must file an Agent-Orange related disability claim before VA will conduct research on a specific ship not on VA's ships list. This requirement also applies to survivors and children with birth defects.

Agent Orange was also sprayed from helicopters and armored personnel carriers, as well as from hand held sprayers.

MACV DATA MANAGEMENT AGENCY

In 1972 I was on my second tour in Vietnam and stationed at the MACV Data Management Agency as an Operations Research Analyst. In the summer, several scientists came over from the National Academy of Science. DMA had been tasked in 1970 to maintain all the flight path data from Operation Ranch Hand, the herbicide spray missions. The database was called HERBS.

The purpose of the visit was to obtain that data and also to plot it out. The agency had a 48" x 72" flatbed plotter and I was assigned to help plot selected data for them. That was to be an interesting task.

Initially, they wanted to plot all flight paths for the period 1965 through 1971 when the spraying ended. That was a joke to me because I knew that the map of RVN would be one huge blob of ink. But we did eventually create a summary for those years shown later herein.

We broke the data into years but that, too, was a mess. The next run was by province and year. For some provinces, we had to break the data down to the district level, comparable to a large school zone. So many flight paths repeated... Here is an example plot of flight paths in 1965.

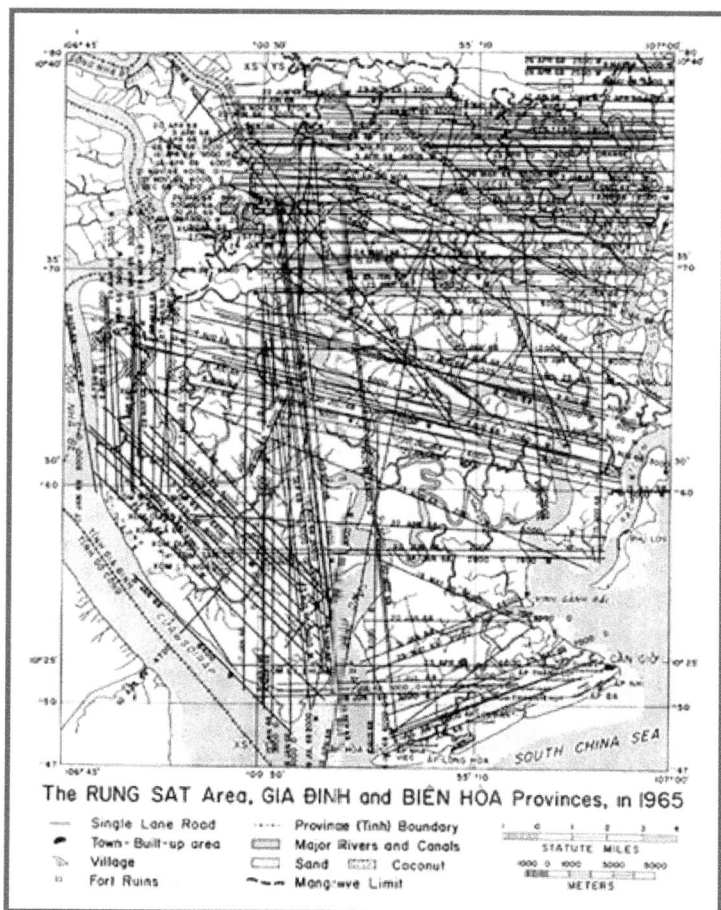

The RUNG SAT Area, GIA ĐINH and BIÊN HÒA Provinces, in 1965

— Single Lane Road   ···· Province (Tinh) Boundary
● Town - Built-up area   ▭ Major Rivers and Canals
▷ Village   ▭ Sand   ▭ Coconut
¤ Fort Ruins   ~~ Mangrove Limit

STATUTE MILES

METERS

Summary Plot 1965 - 1971

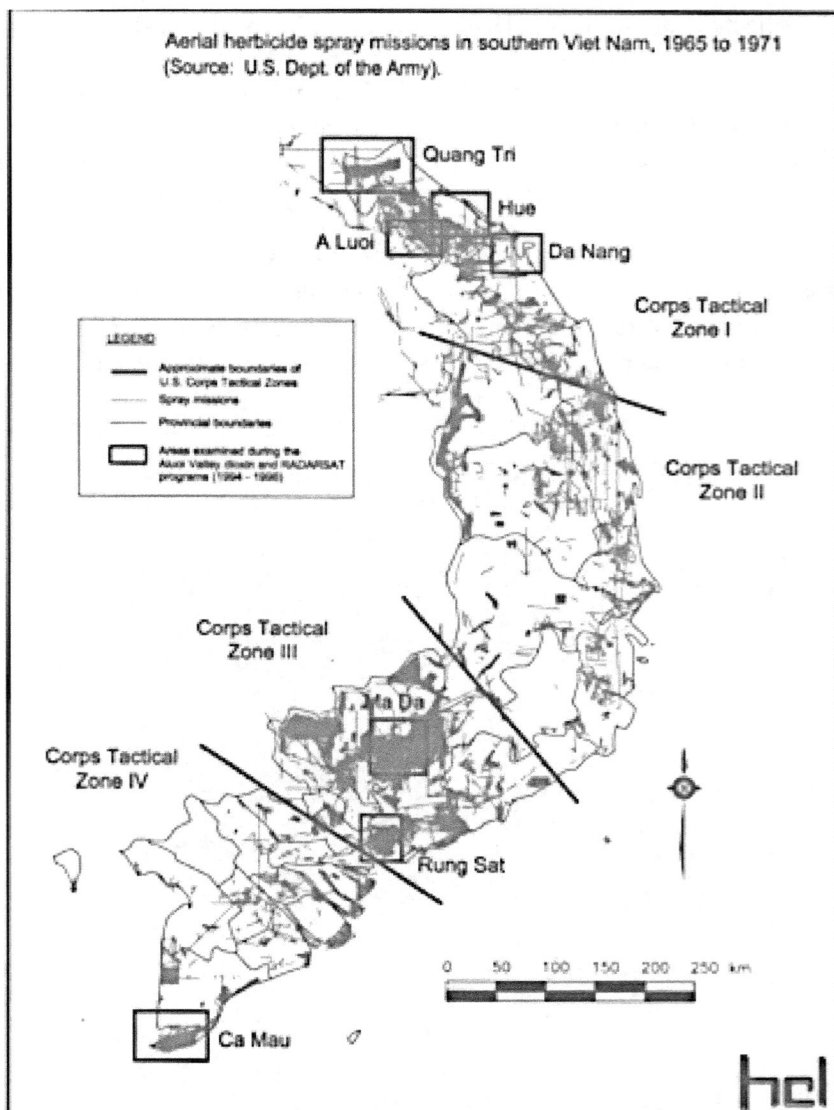

Aerial herbicide spray missions in southern Viet Nam, 1965 to 1971 (Source: U.S. Dept. of the Army).

II Corps Agent Orange Missions

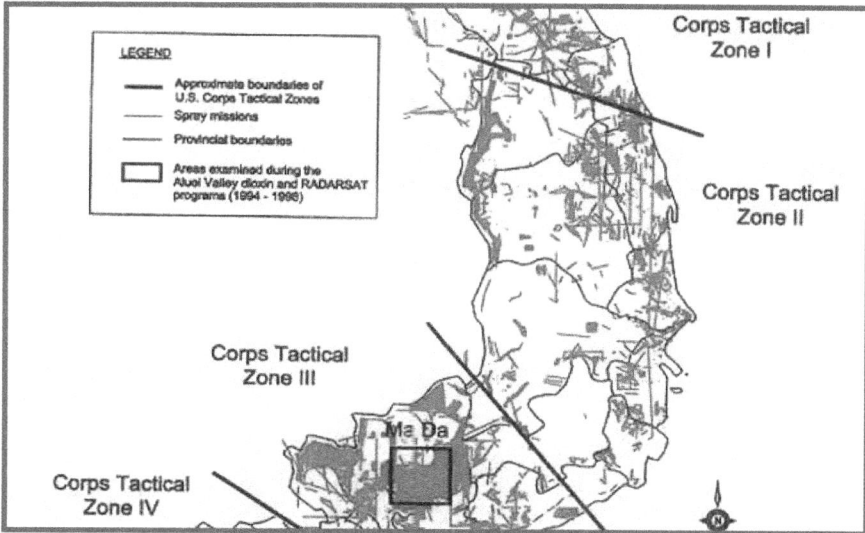

Quantity of Herbicide Sprayed (million gallons)

Year	No. Troops	Orange	White	Blue	Total
1960	900				
1961	3,200				
1962	11,300	NA	NA	NA	
1963	16,300	NA	NA	NA	
1964	23,300	NA	NA	NA	1.2
1965	184,300	0.37	0	0	0.37
1966	385,300	1.64	0.53	0.02	2.19
1967	485,600	3.17	1.33	0.38	4.88
1968	536,100	2.22	2.13	0.28	4.63
1969	475,200	3.25	1.02	0.26	4.53
1970	334,600	0.57	0.22	0.18	0.97
1971	156,800	0	0.01	0	0.01
1972	24,200	0	0	0	0
1973	8250	0	0	0	0
TOTAL		11.22	5.24	1.12	18.85

My Own Agent Orange Story

While Company D was finishing the Phu Hiep AAF, a strange look-ing Huey landed on the western overrun. I walked down to see what was going on and found that the crew was removing a 55-gallon drum from the cargo compartment, apparently to refill the spray unit.

All of a sudden, the drum fell out of the chopper and burst open, flooding the ground with liquid. There was an orange band around the drum, the indicator for Agent Orange. The crew chief told me that they were spraying full strength because it was too hard to dilute the chemi-cal. And besides, we all knew that it wouldn't hurt us. The U.S. Army and U.S. Air Force said so.

The drum contained 10X concentrate. The fluid splashed on my jun-gle boots. Of course I didn't even wash it off. Why would I?

Soon after my return home in 1968, I began to have tingling feelings in my legs. A civilian doctor told me it was because I was tall and had

178

poor circulation in my feet. He checked my circulation and declared it excellent, saying he had no idea why I had a problem. It got worse.

In January of 1992, I was within hours of dying from hyperparathyroidism, which is due to the parathyroid gland(s) going nuts and making too much calcium. A normal male level is 8.5-9.5 and mine was 22.5 on whatever scale they use. The docs managed to flush me out and two weeks later I had surgery to remove the gland. My throat was slit open to get to the spot and while they were in there, a tumor was found on my larynx. Unfortunately, in removing the tumor, the nerve in my right vocal cord was cut, leaving me unable to speak.

The calcium had really messed me up and I was not able to think clearly for many months. Some say it is still so. Anyway, I was forced to sell my business and applied for Social Security Disability. I was told by the clerk that it would take a year and require a lawyer to get it done. But, his also being a Vietnam Vet, he told me, demanded and absolutely insisted that I get my ass to the local VA hospital and get help there.

I was able to get a VA temporary compensation even though it was not service connected (at the time). I also got on the Agent Orange registry and told them about my peripheral neuropathy. Nah, they were not interested in that. Then, later on they started to admit that issue, then stopped, and then started again after a couple of more years.

By this time I was getting lightning like pains in my legs but since that might be good for just 10% disability, I didn't pursue it. I'd already filed for PTSD, which had been creeping out of Pandora's Box for some time, though I was too stupid to see it. In retrospect, I see now how it affected my family many years before I accepted the facts.

After divorcing my first wife, I moved onto a 32 ft sailboat and later I built a 45 ft steel sailboat followed by a second divorce. I lived aboard the two of them for 11 years. I did some charter work and wrote software, but in retrospect, I was really using them as bunkers to avoid a normal life.

After receiving 100% disability for PTSD in 2001 (a 5 year ordeal), it still wasn't over. In 2003 I had injuries on my feet that simply would not heal properly. One took 4-½ months, the other 2-½ years to heal.

In 2007 something wonderful happened. I met and married Heidemarie Olga Margarete Hannemann. She is also know as Heidi. But, as you know, the third time tells the tale and we couldn't be happier.

In 2008 my left leg was amputated below the knee due to circulation problems the VA docs told me were caused by AO.

In 2012 a heart attack required a 6-way bypass. Never heard of one of those before. 6-way?

Today I have no feeling in my right leg from the calf down. My walking is really bad and I will be getting a scooter from the VA before long.

My hands constantly hurt and yet I have almost no feeling in them. Typing this is fun.

And all these things other than PTSD are now Agent Orange related according to the VA. I guesstimate that in excess of $2,000,000 has been spent on me due to that little spill. And, after all this time, I still have chronic emotional problems.

Now, of course, the VA has concluded that ANYONE who was in Vietnam during the war was exposed to Agent Orange. But it wouldn't hurt us. They told us so, even if it did contain known deadly carcinogens, Ah yes, Agent Orange, the gift that keeps on giving. A lasting present from our government.

The VA conducted a study of Vietnam Vets and those who served in the Vietnam Era, but were never in-country. The occurrence of almost every common disease was significantly higher in those who were in-country, even briefly.

There is an official list of diseases below, but if you have a question about something being caused by Agent Orange, go to Google and type the name of the illness and the words AGENT ORANGE. You'll be surprised at what you find and what it may mean to you.

Veterans' Diseases Associated with Agent Orange

The following information is from:
www.publichealth.va.gov/exposures/agentorange/conditions

NOTE: Just because something is not on this list does not mean you cannot get care, and possibly a disability and money from the VA. Again, use Google.

VA assumes that certain diseases can be related to a Veteran's qualifying military service. We call these "presumptive diseases."

VA has recognized certain cancers and other health problems as presumptive diseases associated with exposure to Agent Orange or other herbicides during military service. Veterans and their survivors may be eligible for benefits for these diseases.

AL Amyloidosis

A rare disease caused when an abnormal protein, amyloid, enters tissues or organs

Chronic B-cell Leukemias

A type of cancer which affects white blood cells

Chloracne (or similar acneform disease)

A skin condition that occurs soon after exposure to chemicals and looks like common forms of acne seen in teenagers. Under VA's rating regulations, it must be at least 10 percent disabling within one year of exposure to herbicides.

Diabetes Mellitus Type 2

A disease characterized by high blood sugar levels resulting from the body's inability to respond properly to the hormone insulin

Hodgkin's Disease

A malignant lymphoma (cancer) characterized by progressive enlargement of the lymph nodes, liver, and spleen, and by progressive anemia

Ischemic Heart Disease

A disease characterized by a reduced supply of blood to the heart, that leads to chest pain

Multiple Myeloma

A cancer of plasma cells, a type of white blood cell in bone marrow

Non-Hodgkin's Lymphoma

A group of cancers that affect the lymph glands and other lymphatic tissue

Parkinson's Disease

A progressive disorder of the nervous system that affects muscle movement

Peripheral Neuropathy, Early-Onset

A nervous system condition that causes numbness, tingling, and motor weakness. Under VA's rating regulations, it must be at least 10 percent disabling within one year of herbicide exposure.

Porphyria Cutanea Tarda

A disorder characterized by liver dysfunction and by thinning and blistering of the skin in sun-exposed areas. Under VA's rating regulations, it must be at least 10 percent disabling within one year of exposure to herbicides.

Prostate Cancer

Cancer of the prostate; one of the most common cancers among men

Respiratory Cancers (includes lung cancer)

Cancers of the lung, larynx, trachea, and bronchus

Soft Tissue Sarcomas (other than osteosarcoma, chondrosarcoma, Kaposi's sarcoma, or mesothelioma)

A group of different types of cancers in body tissues such as muscle, fat, blood and lymph vessels, and connective tissues

Children with birth defects

VA presumes certain birth defects in children of Vietnam and Korea Veterans are associated with Veterans' qualifying military service.

Veterans with Lou Gehrig's Disease

VA presumes Lou Gehrig's Disease (amyotrophic lateral sclerosis or ALS) diagnosed in all Veterans who had 90 days or more continuous active military service is related to their service, although ALS is not related to Agent Orange exposure.

Iron Soldiers in Vietnam

Appendix E - Brief History of Vietnam

[1] The Vietnamese first appeared in history as one of many scattered peoples living in what is now South China and Northern Vietnam just before the beginning of the Christian era. According to local tradition, the small Vietnamese kingdom of Au Lac, located in the heart of the Red River Valley, was founded by a line of legendary kings who had ruled over the ancient kingdom of Van Lang for thousands of years. Historical evidence to substantiate this tradition is scanty, but archaeological findings indicate that the early peoples of the Red River delta area may have been among the first East Asians to practice agriculture, and by the 1st century BC they had achieved a relatively advanced level of Bronze Age civilization.

CHINESE INFLUENCE:

In 221 BC the Ch'in dynasty in China completed its conquest of neighboring states and became the first to rule over a united China. The Ch'in Empire, however, did not long survive the death of its dynamic founder, Shih Huang Ti, and the impact of its collapse was soon felt in Vietnam. In the wreckage of the empire, the Chinese commander in the South built his own kingdom of Nam Viet (South Viet; Chinese, Nan Yeh); the young state of Au Lac was included. In 111 BC, Chinese armies conquered Nam Viet and absorbed it into the growing Han Empire. The Chinese conquest had fateful consequences for the future course of Vietnamese history. After briefly ruling through local chieftains, Chinese rulers attempted to integrate Vietnam politically and culturally into the Han Empire. Chinese administrators were imported to replace the local landed nobility. Political institutions patterned after the Chinese model were imposed, and Confucianism became the official ideology. The Chinese language was introduced as the medium of official and literary expression, and Chinese ideographs were adopted as the written form for the Vietnamese spoken language. Chinese art, architecture, and music exercised a powerful impact on their Vietnamese counterparts. Vietnamese resistance to rule by the Chinese was fierce but sporadic. The most famous early revolt took place in AD 39, when two widows of local aristocrats, the Trung sisters, led an uprising against foreign rule. The revolt was briefly successful, and the older sister, Trung Trac, established herself as ruler of an independent state. Chinese armies returned to the attack, however, and in AD 43 Vietnam was reconquered.

INDEPENDENCE:

The Trung sisters' revolt was only the first in a series of intermittent uprisings that took place during a thousand years of Chinese rule in Vietnam. Finally, in 939, Vietnamese forces under Ngo Quyen took advantage of chaotic conditions in China to defeat local occupation troops and set up an independent state. Ngo Quyen's death a few years later ushered in a period of civil strife, but in the early 11th century the first of the great Vietnamese dynasties was founded. Under the astute leadership of several dynamic rulers, the Ly dynasty ruled Vietnam for more than 200 years, from 1010 to 1225. Although the rise of the Ly reflected the emergence of a lively sense of Vietnamese nationhood, Ly rulers retained many of the political and social institutions that had been introduced during the period of Chinese rule. Confucianism continued to provide the foundation for the political institutions of the state. The Chinese civil service examination system was retained as the means of selecting government officials, and although at first only members of the nobility were permitted to compete in the examinations, eventually the right was extended to include most males. The educational system also continued to reflect the Chinese model. Young Vietnamese preparing for the examinations were schooled in the Confucian classics and grew up conversant with the great figures and ideas that had shaped Chinese history. Vietnamese society, however, was more than just a pale reflection of China. Beneath the veneer of Chinese fashion and thought, popular mostly among the upper classes, native forms of expression continued to flourish. Young Vietnamese learned to appreciate the great heroes of the Vietnamese past, many of whom had built their reputation on resistance to the Chinese conquest. At the village level, social mores reflected native forms more than patterns imported from China. Although to the superficial eye Vietnam looked like a "smaller dragon," under the tutelage of the great empire to the North it continued to have a separate culture with vibrant traditions of its own.

THE ECONOMY UNDER THE LY DYNASTY:

Like most of its neighbors, Vietnam was primarily an agricultural state, its survival based above all on the cultivation of wet rice. As in medieval Europe, much of the land was divided among powerful noble families, who often owned thousands of serfs or domestic slaves. A class of landholding farmers also existed, however, and powerful monarchs frequently attempted to protect this class by limiting the power of feudal lords and dividing up their large estates. The Vietnamese economy was not based solely on agriculture. Commerce and manufacturing thrived, and local crafts appeared in regional markets throughout the area. Vietnam never developed into a predominantly commercial nation, however, or became a major participant in regional trade patterns.

TERRITORIAL EXPANSION:

Under the rule of the Ly dynasty and its successor, the Tran (1225-1400), Vietnam became a dynamic force in Southeast Asia. China's rulers, however, had not abandoned their historic objective of controlling the Red River delta, and when the Mongol dynasty came to power in the 13th century, the armies of Kublai Khan attacked Vietnam in an effort to reincorporate it into the Chinese Empire. The Vietnamese resisted with vigor, and after several bitter battles they defeated the invaders and drove them back across the border. While the Vietnamese maintained their vigilance toward the North, an area of equal and growing concern lay to the South. For centuries, the Vietnamese State had been restricted to its heartland in the Red River Valley and adjacent hills. Tension between Vietnam and the kingdom of Champa, a seafaring state along the central coast, appeared shortly after the restoration of Vietnamese independence. On several occasions, Cham armies broke through Vietnamese defenses and occupied the capital near Hanoi. More frequently, Vietnamese troops were victorious, and they gradually drove Champa to the South. Finally, in the 15th century, Vietnamese forces captured the Cham capital south of present-day Da Nang and virtually destroyed the kingdom. For the next several generations, Vietnam continued its historic "march to the South," wiping up the remnants of the Cham Kingdom and gradually approaching the marshy flatlands of the Mekong delta. There it confronted a new foe, the Khmer Empire, which had once been the most powerful state in the region. By the late 16th century, however, it had declined, and it offered little resistance to Vietnamese encroachment. By the end of the 17th century, Vietnam had occupied the lower Mekong delta and began to advance to the West, threatening to transform the disintegrating Khmer State into a mere protectorate.

THE LE DYNASTY:

The Vietnamese advance to the South coincided with new challenges in the North. In 1407 Vietnam was again conquered by Chinese troops. For two decades, the Ming dynasty attempted to reintegrate Vietnam into the empire, but in 1428, resistance forces under the rebel leader Le Loi dealt the Chinese a decisive defeat and restored Vietnamese independence. Le Loi mounted the throne as the first emperor of the Le dynasty. The new ruling house retained its vigor for more than a hundred years, but in the 16th century it began to decline. Power at court was wielded by two rival aristocratic clans, the Trinh and the Nguyen. When the former became dominant, the Nguyen were granted a fiefdom in the South, dividing Vietnam into two separate zones. Rivalry was sharpened by the machinations of European powers newly arrived in Southeast Asia in pursuit of wealth and Christian converts.

By the late 18th century, the Le dynasty was near collapse. Vast rice lands were controlled by grasping feudal lords. Angry peasants-led by the Tay Son brothers-revolted, and in 1789 Nguyen Hue, the ablest of the brothers, briefly restored Vietnam to united rule. Nguyen Hue died shortly after ascending the throne; a few years later Nguyen Anh, an heir to the Nguyen house in the South, defeated the Tay Son armies. As Emperor Gia Long, he established a new dynasty in 1802.

FRENCH INTERVENTION:

A French missionary, Pierre Pigneau de Behaine, had raised a mercenary force to help Nguyen Anh seize the throne in the hope that the new emperor would provide France with trading and missionary privileges, but his hopes were disappointed. The Nguyen dynasty was suspicious of French influence. Roman Catholic missionaries and their Vietnamese converts were persecuted, and a few were executed during the 1830s. Religious groups in France demanded action from the government in Paris. When similar pressure was exerted by commercial and military interests, Emperor Napoleon III approved the launching of a naval expedition in 1858 to punish the Vietnamese and force the court to accept a

French protectorate. The first French attack at Da Nang Harbor failed to achieve its objectives, but a second farther south was more successful, and in 1862 the court at Hue agreed to cede several provinces in the Mekong delta (later called Cochin China) to France. In the 1880s the French returned to the offensive, launching an attack on the North. After severe defeats, the Vietnamese accepted a French protectorate over the remaining territory of Vietnam.

COLONIAL RULE AND RESISTANCE:

The imposition of French colonial rule had met with little organized resistance. The national sense of identity, however, had not been crushed, and anti-colonial sentiment soon began to emerge. Poor economic conditions contributed to native hostility to French rule. Although French occupation brought improvements in transportation and communications, and contributed to the growth of commerce and manufacturing, colonialism brought little improvement in livelihood to the mass of the population. In the countryside, peasants struggled under heavy taxes and high rents. Workers in factories, in coal mines, and on rubber plantations labored in abysmal conditions for low wages. By the early 1920s, nationalist parties began to demand reform and independence. In 1930 the revolutionary Ho Chi Minh formed an Indochinese Communist party. Until World War II started in 1939, such groups labored without success. In 1940, however, Japan demanded and received the right to place Vietnam under military occupation, restricting the local French administration to figurehead authority. Seizing the opportunity, the Communists organized the broad Viet Minh Front and prepared to launch an uprising at the war's end. The Viet Minh (short for Viet Nam Doc Lap Dong Minh, or League for the Independence of Vietnam) emphasized moderate reform and national independence rather than specifically Communist aims. When the Japanese surrendered to the Allies in August 1945, Viet Minh forces arose throughout Vietnam and declared the establishment of an independent republic in Hanoi. The French, however, were unwilling to concede independence and in October drove the Viet Minh and other nationalist groups out of the South. For more than a year the French and the Viet Minh sought a negotiated solution, but the talks, held in France, failed to resolve differences, and war broke out in December 1946.

THE EXPULSION OF THE FRENCH:

The conflict lasted for nearly eight years. The Viet Minh retreated into the hills to build up their forces while the French formed a rival Vietnamese government under Emperor Bao Dai, the last ruler of the Nguyen dynasty, in populated areas along the coast. Viet Minh forces lacked the strength to defeat the French and generally restricted their activities to guerrilla warfare. In 1953-1954 the French fortified a base at Dien Bien Phu. After months of siege and heavy casualties, the Viet Minh overran the fortress in a decisive battle. As a consequence, the French government could no longer resist pressure from a war-weary populace at home and in June 1954 agreed to negotiations to end the war. At a conference held in Geneva the two sides accepted an interim compromise to end the war. They divided the country at the 17th parallel, with the Viet Minh in the North and the French and their Vietnamese supporters in the South. To avoid permanent partition, a political protocol was drawn up, calling for national elections to reunify the country two years after the signing of the treaty.

PARTITION:

After Geneva, the Viet Minh in Hanoi refrained from armed struggle and began to build a Communist society. In the southern capital, Saigon, Bao Dai soon gave way to a new regime under the staunch anti-Communist president Ngo Dinh Diem. With diplomatic support from the United States, Diem refused to hold elections and attempted to destroy Communist influence in the South. By 1959, however, Diem was in trouble. His unwillingness to tolerate domestic opposition, his alleged favoritism of fellow Roman Catholics, and the failure of his social and economic programs seriously alienated key groups in the populace and led to rising unrest. The Communists decided it was time to resume their revolutionary war.

THE AMERICAN WAR:

In the fall of 1963, Diem was overthrown and killed in a coup launched by his own generals. In the political confusion that followed, the security situation in South Vietnam continued to deteriorate, putting the Communists within reach of victory. In early 1965, to prevent the total collapse of the Saigon regime, U.S. President Lyndon Johnson approved regular intensive bombing of North Vietnam and the dispatch of U.S. combat troops into the South. The U.S. intervention caused severe problems for the Communists on the battlefield and compelled them to send regular units of the North Vietnamese army into the South. It did not persuade them to abandon the struggle, however, and in 1968, after the bloody Tet offensive shook the new Saigon regime of President Nguyen Van Thieu to its foundations, the Johnson administration decided to pursue a negotiated settlement. Ho Chi Minh died in 1969 and was succeeded by another leader of the revolution, Le Duan. The new U.S. president, Richard Nixon, continued Johnson's policy while gradually withdrawing U.S. troops. In January 1973 the war temporarily came to an end with the signing of a peace agreement in Paris. The settlement provided for the total removal of remaining U.S. troops, while Hanoi tacitly agreed to accept the Thieu regime in preparation for new national elections. The agreement soon fell apart, however, and in early 1975 the Communists launched a military offensive. In six weeks, the resistance of the Thieu regime collapsed, and on April 30 the Communists seized power in Saigon.

THE SOCIALIST REPUBLIC OF VIETNAM:

In 1976 the South was reunited with the North in a new Socialist Republic of Vietnam. The conclusion of the war, however, did not end the violence. Border tension with the Communist government in Cambodia escalated rapidly after the fall of Saigon, and in early 1979 the Vietnamese invaded Cambodia and installed a pro-Vietnamese government. A few weeks later, Vietnam was itself attacked by its Communist neighbor and erstwhile benefactor, China. In the mid-1980s, Vietnamese troops were stationed in Cambodia and Laos. Vietnam substantially reduced its forces in Laos during 1988 and withdrew virtually all its troops from Cambodia by September 1989. Within Vietnam, postwar economic and social problems were severe, and reconstruction proceeded slowly. Efforts to collectivize agriculture and nationalize business aroused hostility in the South. Disappointing harvests and the absorption of resources by the military further retarded Vietnam's recovery. In the early 1990s, the government encouraged foreign investment and sought to improve relations with the United States.

Recent policies, trade agreements, and treaties have positioned Vietnam for peace, growth and prosperity in the twenty-first century.

[1] Brief History In Vietnam, www.vietventures.com, 2000-2015, used with permission

Appendix F - Military Slang and Abbreviations

If, as Emerson said, language is the archive of history, then U.S. soldiers in Vietnam were writing history with words as well as weapons.

So many slang terms, Vietnamese words and specialized usages were used by U.S. soldiers in Vietnam that language poses a bit of a problem to the new man coming over. Until he picks up the current slang, he is marked as a recent arrival.

With the Vietnam-bound replacement in mind, the Army Times compiled the following list of non-standard terms used in Vietnam.

The list has been modified and copyrighted by John Podlaski to include pictures. See https://cherrieswriter.wordpress.com/2014/02/13/military-speak-during-the-vietnam-war. Used with permission with my own modifications and additions.

50 foot roll of flight line: Non-existent item that chopper groups usually send new recruits to look for.

Ao dai ("owzeye"): The native costume of Vietnamese women. It has a mandarin collar and is very tight in the bodice with the skirt split to the waist. Worn over loose silk pants.

AO: Acronym for Area of Operations – terrain assigned to specific units — their responsibility to locate and kill enemy soldiers within that area.

APC: Armored Personnel Carrier – tracked vehicle used by mechanized units for squad sized patrols.

Arc-Light: Code name for B-52 strike missions — used as close air support against enemy base camps, troop concentrations and supplies. Releasing their bombs from high in the stratosphere, the B-52s could neither be seen nor heard from the ground. B-52s were instrumental in nearly wiping out enemy concentrations besieging Khe Sanh in 1968 and An Loc and Kontum in 1972.

Aussie: Australian Soldier and America's ally

Assholes and elbows: in a hurry; quickly.

Ba mui ba (Beer 33"): vietnamese beer. A French beer originally. Rumored to be spiked with formaldehyde due to inoperative French era pasteurization equipment. If you start getting a headache, stop drinking Ba mui ba.

Baby San: GI reference to village children (male and female)

Ba muoi lam ("baa-mooee-lahm): Vietnamese for the number 35. Means the same as "butterfly;" a playboy.

Base Camp Commando: Soldiers assigned to the main base camp

Beaucoup: From the French. In Vietnam it can mean many, much, big, huge, very, etc.

Betel nut ("beetle nut"): The leaves or root of the betel palm, which are mildly narcotic and are chewed by many Vietnamese, especially aged women, to relieve the pain of diseased gums. The cumulative effect of years of betel nut chewing is to totally blacken the teeth.

Biscuit Bitches: Derogatory term referencing Donut Dollies

Birds: Helicopters or choppers

Blooper: M79 Grenade Launcher. Also referred as Thumper

BOHICA: Acronym meaning – Bend Over Here It Comes Again

Bong Son Bomber: Giant sized marijuana cigarette

Boom-boom: Slang for having sex

Boom-Boom Girl: Prostitute

Boondocks (boonies): Isolated backcountry.

Bouncing Betty Mines: The German S-mine (Schrapnellmine in German) is the best-known version of a class of mines known as bounding mines. When triggered, these mines launch into the air and then detonate at about waist height.

Broken arrow: Universal code meaning that a ground unit or camp is being overrun and to send all available assets. Also referred as a serviceman who tried to be a straight arrow and failed. (See straight arrow.)

Brothers-in-Arms: All Veterans united – having a special bond between them.

BUFFF: Big Ugly Flying Fat Fuckers – ref. B52 bombers. Also referred as "Dump trucks" in northern I-Corps.

Bullet Catcher: A safety device for mini guns that was removed before flight. Also slang for the front seater in a Cobra.

Bush: Field, jungle, boonies, Indian country — any combination of these words describes hostile areas outside of firebases and basecamps

Butter Bar: Slang reference for a Second Lieutenant – also called LT (ell-tee)

Butterfly: Playboy.

Buy the farm: To be killed. Sometimes "buy the six-by-three farm."

Bravo-Zulu (BZ): Well Done!

C-4: Plastic explosive

Cam on "cahm oon"): Vietnamese for "thank you."

Canh Sat ("cahn zaht"): White mice or Vietnamese Police

Can Kuk or Con Kuk: Civilian ID card

Care package: Box of goodies sent to soldiers by their family or friends — usually containing cookies, candy, condiments to flavor c-rations, home newspapers, coffee, gum and any other treats that can be thought of. Infantry soldiers in the field do not receive these because of the added weight and they are stored at the firebase supply upon their return.

CG: Commanding General.

Chao co (ong) (em) (pronounced "chow coh (ohm) (em)"): Vietnamese for hello or good-bye, Miss (Sir) (to a child, animal or very close friend).

Cheap charlie: Anyone, especially a U.S. serviceman, who does not waste his money. (See "plenty cheap charlie.")

Chieu Hoi ("chew hoyee"): the Vietnamese-administered "Open Arms" program for defecting enemy soldiers. (See "Hoi Chanh.")

Cherry: designation for new replacement from the states. Also referred as FNG (fucking new guy), fresh meat and new citizens

Chop-chop: Food, or eat – used primarily by Vietnamese. Some troops used the words to 'hurry up."

CIDG: Civilian Irregular Defense Group. Friendly indigenous forces, usually organized and led by Army Special Forces teams

Cluster Fuck: Nothing is going right, congested or bunched up.

Coka: Vietnamese pronunciation of "Coke."

Coup qualified: Very old Viet hands, and only those who served in Saigon during a violent overthrow of a Vietnamese government, are said to be "coup qualified."

Cowboy: A Vietnamese ruffian — usually riding a motor bike and swiping jewelry from those they pass by.

Crow's foot: A four-pointed booby trap device which, when thrown, will land with one point up.

C's: "C" rations.

Cyclo: Three-wheeled motorized conveyance with a seat on the front.

Daisy Cutter: Shell or bomb fitted with a fuse extension to provide detonation 1-6 feet above ground, minimizing the cratering effect and maximizing the blast effect. Used with large bombs (2000 lb) and 6-foot daisy cutter fuses to create an instant clearing in dense jungle for an LZ.

Day Off: See "khong lau."

Deuce-and-a-half: 2 1/2 ton truck.

Dep lam ("dep lahm"): Vietnamese for "too pretty [or handsome)."

Dep qua ("dep whah"): Vietnamese for "pretty."

Dep trai ("dep cheye"): Vietnamese for "handsome."

DEROS: Acronym used in Vietnam to determine the date a soldier can go home "Date Eligible Return from Overseas"

Di di (mau) ("dee-dee (maow)"): Vietnamese for "go away (fast) or "haul ass"

Dien cai dao ("dee-in-kee-daow"): Vietnamese for "crazy in the head."

Diddy-bop: Term used to criticize the way a person or group is walking, (i.e. shuffling to a tune, not paying attention, too carefree), swagger

Diggers: Australian infantry soldiers

Dinky Dau: Slang for crazy or completely nuts

Disneyland Far East: Hq building of the U.S. Military Assistance Command Vietnam. Name is derived from "Disneyland East" (the Pentagon).

DMZ: Demilitarized zone – Neutral area separating North Vietnam from South Vietnam

Donut Dollies: Young women from the Red Cross who were stationed in many of the rear areas and managed service clubs for the troops. Their jobs were to motivate and entertain…some were known to visit troops in desolate areas out in the bush.

Dolphin: a five-ton tractor. (See "guppy.")

Don't mean nuthin: Coined by G.I.'s in Vietnam. A reverse coping expression indicating that it means everything and I'm about to lose it. Usually used to dismiss witnessing or experiencing something so horrific that it can't be comprehended by the psyche. Alternately used as an expression of relief that one has avoided being killed even if they are injured or maimed.

Dung lai (pronouneed "zoong lye"): Vietnamese for "halt" or "stop."

Duster: A truck or track armed with twin 40mm cannon.

Dustoff: The medevac z system. These brave pilots often placed themselves at risk by landing during a firefight with the enemy to pick up wounded soldiers.

ETS: Acronym used by the military to determine the date ending a soldiers term of service "End Time of Service"

FAC: Forward air controller. A light plane pilot who directs air strikes and artillery fire from the air.

Fallopian tubing for inside the turrets of tanks: Prank used by tankers to send Cherries on a wild goose chase

Fast Mover: – Slang for a Jet Fighter.

FIGMO: Acronym for "Finally I got my orders." Especially in "figmo chart", a shorttimer's calendar, usually a drawing of an undraped female form, with numbered sections which are filled in, one each day, as the shorttimer keeps track of days to go.

Fini: From the French. Vietnamese meanings include through, finished, depart (as in, "When you fini Vietnam, GI?") and even kill (as is, "She fini him with knife.").

Fire-For-Effect: The continuous firing of a battery's cannons, sustained until a 'cease-fire' or 'check-fire' is called.

Fire in the hole!: Warning that explosives are about to be detonated.

First Light: The time of nautical twilight when the sun is 12 degrees below the horizon.

Flower seeker: A term used, especially in the Vietnamese press, to describe a man in search of a prostitute.

FNG: Fucking New Guy)designation for new replacement from the states. Also referred as Cherry, fresh meat and new citizens

FO: Forward Observer, traveled with the infantry and coordinated arty missions, or an airborne FAC.

FOD: Foreign Object Damage

Foo Gas: (sometimes contracted to fougasse and may be spelled foo gas) is a type of mine which uses an explosive charge to project burning liquid onto a target

Frag: Fragmentation grenade. Also refers to the murder of fellow soldiers in retaliation for an action or order that resulted in somebody getting hurt or killed. This usually happened by tossing a live grenade into a latrine or barracks occupied by the individual.

Freedom bird: Commercial jet aircraft which flies returning servicemen to the U.S.

FSA: Forward support area (or activity); one-stop service base established by logistical units near an operation or forward base camp.

FSB: Acronym for Fire Support Base. A fire support base was originally a temporary firing base for artillery, although many evolved into more permanent bases.

FUBAR: Acronym for Fucked Up Beyond Any Recognition

Fugazi: – Completely out of whack, fucked up, screwy. This term originated during the Vietnam War and experienced limited use by civilians.

Grunt: An infantryman, also called "Ground pounders"

Gooks: Derogatory term referencing VC or NVA soldiers. Also called: "Chuck", "Charlie", "Dinks" and "Slopes"

Gooks in the wire: Alarm for Enemy soldiers trying to infiltrate a basecamp or firebase.

Greased: Killed also referred as zapped and bought the farm

Gunship: Armed helicopter with the primary mission of fire support.

Guppy: A stake-and-platform trailer of the type pulled by a five-ton tractor. (See "dolphin.")

Hanoi Hannah: the Tokyo Rose of the Vietnam war. She played good jazz on the radio late at night.

Hard Truck / Gun Truck: Provides support to convoys traveling through known hostile territory

Headman: The boss man of a local community. His word is usually law.

Hero: Reference to those having served in Vietnam, circa 2014

High Angle Fire: Artillery trajectory wherein the shell travels higher than its distance down range. Used for firing over intervening mountains, etc, inherently less accurate than low angle fire (standard) due to shell ballistics and wind effects.

Ho Chi Minh sandals: Sandals made from worn-out truck tires. Also referred to as "Ho Chi Minh Road Sticks"

Ho Chi Minh trail: The complex of jungle paths through Laos and Cambodia which serves as the principle Viet Cong and NVA supply route.

Hog / Pig: M60 Machine Gun primarily used by Americans. Uses 7.62 x 51 NATO rounds which are longer and similar to the enemy's Russian made AK-47 (7.62 x 39) these rounds are not interchangeable and cannot be fired from the opposing weapon.

Hoi Chanh (pronounced "hoyee cahn"): A returnee. An enemy soldier who voluntarily gave himself up. Many were employed by the Vietnamese government or the U.S. Army. Referred to as "Kit Carson Scout" by infantry units.

Hong Kong Rubber: The variety used by many Vietnamese girls to help them put on a good front. Standing joke among Vietnam-based servicemen: "And to think I could have bought stock in Hong Kong Rubber when it was down to 31."

Howard Johnson's: Any of a multitude of pushcart vendors selling food in the street.

Howitzer: An artillery cannon capable of both High-angle and Low-Angle fire. The 105mm howitzer was the most commonly deployed type in Vietnam, weighed about 5,000 lbs, and could fire a shell 11,500 meters (7 miles) at a rate of 3 rounds per minute. The 155mm howitzer was either a 2-wheeled, towed cannon (M114) or a tracked, self propelled weapon (M109-SP), weighed 12,700lbs (M114) or 52,460lbs (M109-SP) and could fire its shells 14,600 meters (9 miles), at 1 round per minute. The 81-Inch howitzer was a self-propelled cannon weighing 58,500lbs and could fire 16,800 meters (10.4 miles), at 1 round every 2 minutes.

Humping: Walking from one location to another while carrying full rucksacks and supplies - routes can be through dense jungle, along paths or trails, through streams and rice paddies and sometimes uphill / downhill on very steep slopes. To march; to carry; to be burdened with.

Idiot stick: A rifle or2. the curved yoke used by Vietnaese, usually old women or children, to carry two rice baskets, water buckets or what have you, one hung from each end of the yoke. Sometimes referred to as a "Dummy stick."

Incoming! (always exclamatory): "Hit the dirt!" Warning for aerial barrage (mortars, artillery, rockets, etc.) from enemy soldiers.

In-country: in Vietnam.

Jack Benny plus 10: Mr. Benny always claimed to be 39 years old. Pilots, when wanting to adjust a radio frequency may reference JB and a number. i.e. Jack Benny up 10.5 would reference frequency 49.5…same would apply for down plus a number to subtract.

Jesus Nut: Main connector which holds a helicopter rotor in place

Jody: Make believe person who is said to be romancing your wife or girlfriend while you are training or stationed oversees.

Khong lau (pronounced "kohng laow"): Vietnamese for "nevah hoppen."

KIWIS: New Zealander Soldier and America's ally

Lai day: (pronounced "lye dye"): Vietnamese for "come here."

Lam on: (pronounced "lahm oon"): Vietnamese for "please."

Lanyard grease: Prank used to send Cherries on a wild goose chase

LBFM: Has to do with indigenous females and the sexual favor they provide (use your imagination on this one)…SF guys don't want to spill the beans.

LBJ:. Long Binh Jail; the USARV Stockade, or Camp Long Binh Junction, home of the 90th Replacement Bn, through which most individual replacements are processed.

Left Handed Monkey Wrench: A non-existent tool. Often the object of fruitless searches undertaken by recruits at the behest of more experienced service members.

Lifers: Career soldiers

Lima charlie: international phonetic alphabet words for "LC", short for "loud and clear" in Army radio parlance.

Loach: The nimble little Hughes OH-6 Cayuse served extensively with U.S. Army forces in the Vietnam War

L.T.: pronounced ell-tee which was short for lieutenant…most infantry officers accepted this out in the bush.

LRRP: Long Range Reconnaissance Patrol (4 – 8 men) that worked deep in enemy controlled areas to gather intelligence.

LZ: Landing zone…anywhere a helicopter can land

Mad Minute: Order given for all bunkers to shoot across their front for one minute…used to test fire weapons and also enemy harassment. Out in the field, the leader may order the troops on line and have them shoot into a suspicious area they plan to enter – called Recon By Fire

Malayan gate: A booby trap device which depends on a ful-crum for action and usually employs spikes as the killing device. Devised by Malay communists during their unsuccessful 10 year fight against the British.

Mama San: GI reference to all older Vietnamese women

Mau len (pronounced "maow len"): Vietnamese for fast, or speed. As in, "Let's mau len it up a bit, Papasan."

Meat Wagon: Slang for an ambulance, or any other medical emergeny vehicle

Medevac: Short for medical evacuation.

Mike Boat: Landing craft, mechanized (LCM8) used to carry troops.

Military General Orders:

1. To take charge of this post and all government property in view.

2. To walk my post in a military manner, keeping always on the alert, and observing everything that takes place within sight or hearing.

3. To report all violations of orders I am instructed to enforce.

4. To repeat all calls from posts more distant from the guard house than my own.

5. To quit my post only when properly relieved.

6. To receive, obey, and pass on to the sentry who relieves me all orders from the commanding officer, field officer of the day, officer of the day, and officers and petty officers of the watch.

7. To talk to no one except in line of duty.

8. To give the alarm in case of fire or disorder.

9. To call the petty officer of the watch in any case not covered by instructions.

10. To salute all officers and all colors and standards not cased.

11. To be especially watchful at night, and during the time for challenging, to challenge all persons on or near my post, and to allow no one to pass without proper authority.

Mine Magnet: Any armored vehicle (APC, tank, etc.)

Monopoly Money: MPC – Military Payment Certificates used by the military in Vietnam. Greenbacks were illegal.

Mortar: Crew served, muzzle loading, high angle cannon. 4.2 Inch mortars fired projectiles similar to the 105mm howitzer, HE, WP, Illum, etc. Used primarily for fire missions at ranges too short for howitzers (2-3 Km).

MOS: Military occupation specialty.

M.U.L.E. : Multi Utility Light Equipment – small motorized cart used to carry equipment and supplies within firebases

Numbah-one GI: Serviceman who spends a good deal of money on the Vietnamese economy.

Numbah-ten GI: Serviceman who spends little money on the Vietnamese economy, or one who refuses to make a proposed purchase.

Numbah-ten thousand: Absolutely the worst of the lot

Nuoc mam ("noouk mom"): Vietnamese national dish; fermented fish sauce.

Old Boots / Old Timers: Those soldiers who have been in country for a while – others look to them for advice and direction due to their experience

Papa San: GI reference to all older Vietnamese men

PDQ: Acronym for "on the double: or "in a hurry", pretty damn quick.

Pedicab: A foot-powered cyclo.

Plastic: Type of explosives favored by sappers. As in, "I was in the middle of a steak at the Hoa Lu BEQ when they found 200 pounds of plastic behind the bar, so I stuck my fork in my steak and di-di-maued."

Plenty cheap charlie: One who wastes even less money than an ordinary cheap charlie.

Prairie Fire: Code word used by MACVSOG to identify recon ops into Laos (previously known as Shining Brass) and it was also used by helicopter pilots flying in support of SOG's Recon A team was in imminent danger of being overrun, or was compromised and on the run – the exfil of SOG-assets in an emergency.

P's: Piasters; basic Vietnamese monetary unit.

PSP: Perforated Steel Planking – standardized, perforated steel matting material originally developed by the United States shortly before World War II, primarily for the rapid construction of temporary runways and landing strips. First Use in November 1941. The material was also used in the Korean and Vietnam Wars where its common name is pierced (or perforated) steel planking or PSP. A runway two hundred feet wide and 5000 feet (1500 m) long could be created within two days by a small team of engineers.

Puff: Originally "Puff the Magic Dragon"; a C-47 armed with miniguns or other rapid fire weapons. It is said that if firing while flying over a football field, a bullet will hit every square foot of the field. Also called "Spooky" or "Dragon Ships'.

Punji stick: Sharpened stake, usually bamboo, planted in the ground with the point sticking up. Often used in booby traps and often employed with the point smeared with feces as a poisoning element.

Quan Canh (pronounced "kwuhn kein"): Vietnamese military police.

RA: Acronym for Regular Army (those who joined voluntarily)

Rats: An "in" term used by some Saigon warriors for "white mice."

REAL LIFE (always capitalized): civilian life. As in, "What do you do in Real Life, Jonesie?"

Redball: The system used in Vietnam to expedite delivery of critical supplies and repair parts, or Camp Redball, a small base camp near Go Vap, a Saigon suburb.

Re-Up Bird: Blue Eared Barbet – bird whose song sounds like "Re UP" to those soldiers in the jungle

REFRAD: Acronym for Released From Active Duty

REMF: Acronym for Rear Echelon Military Force…derogatory designation is Rear Echelon Mother Fucker

RF/PF: Acronym for Regional Forces/Popular Forces.

Rice wine: An alcoholic drink, very inexpensive, made from rice. Usually tastes like kerosene.

RIKKI-TIK: To do quickly…"move out rikki-tik"

Rog: (pronounced "rahj"): Short for "Roger", the radio term for "I read (understand) your transmission." Also, in the expression, "That's a Rog, Baby" (That's right).

Roger That /Roger-Roger: Term used by Army aviators indicating that the transmission was received and understood.

ROK: Marines from Korea – allies with U.S. to fight communism

Rotor Wash: Non-existent item. New troops are sent to supply to look for a can of this.

Round: Bullet or artillery or mortar shell.

Round eye: Caucasian woman.

RPG: Rocket Propelled Grenade. Weapon of choice by VC / NVA for attacks on armor and against sandbagged bunkers.

Ruff-Puffs: Derogatory term used by Americans to the RF/PF troops. South Vietnamese Regional Forces were roughly akin to militias. Recruited locally, they fell into two broad groups – Regional Forces and Popular Forces. During the early 60's the Regional Forces manned the country-wide output system and defended critical points, such as bridges and ferries. There were some 9,000 such positions, half of them in the Mekong Company D region. In 1964, the Regional Forces were integrated into the Army of the Republic of Vietnam (ARVN) and placed under the command of the Joint General Staff.

Saigon Tea: Colored water (sometimes soda) purchased in thimble-size glasses as the price of a hostess' company in a bar or nightclub. The hostess gets a commission, and she can drink as many as the customer can buy, as fast as he can buy them.

Saigon warrior: Drugstore soldier, especially one who serves or has served in Saigon.

Same-Same: First heard it during the Vietnam War in the 60s. It's still used quite extensively throughout Vietnam by Vietnamese as well as Australian and U.S. ex-servicemen. Having said that, I am noticing younger generations of tourists becoming quite enamoured by the same same.

How do you feel?

Same same yesterday. What's the difference between these two beers.

Same same. All Vietnamese same same... black hair, brown eyes.

Shake 'n Bake: Soldiers who earn sergeant stripes after specialized training prior to arrival in Vietnam. Program was established to help fill-in leadership holes within the ranks during the war.

Shaming: Goofing off or getting by with the least amount of effort.

Shit on a Shingle: Slang for a piece of toast with chipped beef and gravy.

Shitters: Outhouse like enclosures – usually 3 or 6 holes (3 and 3 across from one another) cut in a wooden plank and suspended over 55 gallon half barrels. Usually in firebases – no place for modesty

Shit burning: Day-long ritual at firebases where filled half-barrels are pulled out from the enclosures and replaced with empties. A soldier or Vietnamese is assigned to burn all the waste with a mixture of kerosene and diesel fuel.

So mot ("sah maht"): Vietnamese for "numbah one", the best.

So mudi (sah mooee"): Vietnamese for "numbah 10", the worst.

Sapper: a soldier, especially an enemy soldier, whose job is to blow things up.

Shithook: Boeing CH-47 Chinook helicopter

Siesta: Vietnam quits from noon to 2:30 p.m. This period of each day is known as siesta.

Short: Term signifying that the individual's tour of duty is almost completed – usually less than 100 days. Short timers carry notched walking sticks, colorful calendars…most compare the last 30 days in country with their Cherry days and become extremely paranoid and not wanting to take risks anymore.

Shell-WP: Shell carrying white phosphorus. Explodes and scatters burning pieces of phosphorus over the target to cause fire damage, or may be used for the screening effect of the dense white smoke produced by burning phosphorus.

Shell-Smoke: Carried a grey smoke mixture; used almost exclusively as a marking round with an airburst fuse. Produced a ball of smoke on detonation.

Shell-Illum: Shell carrying a parachute flare for lighting up an area at night. ILLUM always burst at altitude with a 'soft' ejection charge igniting and pushing the flare out of the rear of the shell body. The flare fell slowly on its parachute, providing illumination, while the shell body traveled downrange and the base plate of the shell fell somewhat backward along the flight path. Firing ILLUM required the FDC to predict all three-impact points in order to prevent injury to friendlies due to falling metal.

207

Sort Round: Artillery round which falls short of its target.

SHOT!: Radio signal from battery to FO that his shells are in flight.

Shrapnel: high velocity metal fragments thrown off by an exploding shell. The Beehive round which projected steel darts superseded the older shrapnel or 'canister' shell, which ejected steel balls toward the enemy, in Vietnam.

Sit-Rep: Short for Situation Report. Field units and firebase bunkers are normally contacted on an hourly basis by the company / battalion radio operator. If nothing is going on, normally answered – negative sit-rep. If in hostile territory, a negative response is interpreted as breaking squelch twice in a row on the radio.

Slick: Transport helicopter.

Slick Sleeves: Bare armed Private E-2.

Soften Up An LZ: Artillery fire on a potentially dangerous LZ prior to troops arriving by helicopter

Splash!: Radio signal from battery to FO that his shells will impact in 10 seconds.

SNAFU: Situation Normal All Fucked Up

Steam and Cream: Steam room or massage parlors operated by prostitutes…pay for happy endings.

STIF: Acronym for "Saigon Tea Is Fini", an organization formed to combat increases in the price of Saigon Tea. Members would fill a bar which had raised its prices and sit sipping beer without buying Tea. Their "drink-ins" met with limited success.

Straight arrow: Serviceman who remains faithful to his wife or Stateside girl friend throughout his Vietnam tour. (See "broken arrow.")

TARFU: Acronym for Things Are Really Fucked Up

Tarmac: Material used for surfacing roads or other outdoor areas, consisting of crushed rock mixed with tar. It is often used to describe the apron or runway of an airport.

The 'Nam: Vietnam.

The Pill: Any one of several types of tablets taken weekly by all servicemen in Vietnam as a defense against most types of malaria.

The WORLD (always capitalized): The USA. As in, "Where you from back in The World, Sarge?"

Thunder Road: Highway 1 – main north / south highway.

Ti ti ("tee-tee"): Vietnamese for "small."

Toe Poppers: U.S. mine meant to maim an individual when stepping on them. The M14 mine, looked like a small, thick disc that was olive drab in color, 2.2 inches in diameter and 1.5 inches in height. It contained 1 ounce of Tetryl explosive to make up its 3.5 ounce weight. This lightness came from its mostly plastic construction, and, to set it off, required a pressure of between 20 to 35 pounds. The mine could be placed in a shallow hole, under a leaf or in the open if in a hurry. Special Forces teams often used this last tactic when breaking contact or protecting a perimeter at night.

Toi khong biet ("toy kohng bee-ech"): Vietnamese for "I don't know" or "I don't understand."

Toi yen em (nhieu lam) ("toy you em (nyoo lahm)"): Vietnamese for "I love you (too much)."

Tomorrow: Never make a date for "tomorrow" with a Vietnamese girl. "'Tomorrow' nevah come in Vietnam, GI."

Tracks: Vehicle with tracks that carry howitzer or other large guns, also APC's.

Troi oi ("choyee oyee"): An emphatic expression in Vietnamese which can mean just about anything the user wants it to mean. Troi duc oi (choyee duck oyee) is the same expression more emphatically stated.

Tunnel Rat or "Rat": A soldier trained to enter enemy enclosed spaces like tunnel systems to search them and eliminate and/or capture any occupants.

Tube of Super Torque: Non existent article – newbies are sent to locate this item within chopper groups

Two-Stepper: Bamboo pit viper – said to kill a person within two steps after being bitten.

Un-Ass: To move immediately or leave one's current position.

Upcountry: any place north of the Saigon-Long Binh-Bien Hoa area.

U.S.: Acronym meaning Unwilling Service (referring to Draftees)

USArmy: Acronym for U Sonsabitches Are Ruining My Youth

U.S. ARMY: Acronym for Uncle Sam Ain't Released Me Yet

USELESS: Homonym pun on USIS, the United States Information Service.

"V": V-100 Armored Car made by Cadillac and used as convoy escort

White mice: The Canh Sat; the Vietnamese national police force. Its members wear white shirts.

White space: The most prevalent element on the front pages of the best Vietnamese newspapers when censorship is in effect, which is usually.

Wickham trolley: An armored railroad locomotive of the type developed by the British during the Malayan rebellion.

Willie Pete: White phosphorous

Xau lam ("saow lahm"): Vietnamese for "numbah ten thousand" (indescribably bad.).

Xin loi ("sin loyee"): Vietnamese for "Sorry 'bout that."

Yard: Short for Montagnard, a French word meaning; "mountaineer." Member of any one of a number of semi-nomadic, aboriginal tribes which live in the mountains of Vietnam.

You Bam Bam: Another Vietnamese saying used to tell GI's they were "Crazy", similar to "Dinky Dau."

Zap: To kill or seriously wound.

Zero-dark-thirty: Pre-dawn; early.

Zippo: Brand of lighter most commonly carried during the war. Soldiers engraved them to show their personality.

Zippo: Any tracked vehicle or boat that has an attached flame thrower.